We are not going to be able to operate our Spaceship Earth successfully nor for much longer unless we see it as a whole spaceship and our fate as common. It has to be everybody or nobody....

—R. Buckminster Fuller

There are no passengers on Spaceship Earth, we are all crew.

—Marshall McLuhan

Once a photograph of the Earth, taken from outside, is available...a new idea as powerful as any in history will be let loose.

—Jim Hoyle, Astronomer, 1948

You develop an instant global consciousness, a people orientation, an intense dissatisfaction with the state of the world, and a compulsion to do something about it. From out there on the moon, international politics looks so petty.

—Edgar Mitchell, Apollo 14 Astronaut

We should try to be the parents of our future rather than the offspring of our past.

—Miguel de Unamuno, Spanish essayist
  and philosopher

D0831467

THIS SPACESHIP EARTH

DAVID HOULE / TIM RUMAGE

PHOTO: NASA

Copyright © 2015 David Houle + Timothy Rumage

Published by David Houle & Associates

ISBN:
(paperback): 978-0-9905635-3-2
(epub): 78-0-9905635-4-9
(mobi): 978-0-9905635-5-6

Printed in the United States of America

First Edition

 David Houle & Associates

To Victoria, as always, with love and gratitude.

To Christopher and to Jordan as being crew on TSE will be central for the rest of your lives.

To R. Buckminster Fuller and Marshall McLuhan for instilling in me the concept of Earth as a spaceship, decades ago.

To everyone who is already living and acting as crew.

David

To Sheryl–artist, designer, spouse, partner, collaborator without whom many of life's (mis)adventures would have had less joy.

To MacKenZie whose being constantly reminds me of the need to Face the Future and do/be better.

To Ian McHarg and Rachel Carson whose writings helped me see differently.

To my students who demonstrate the value of Art and Design in creating inventive solutions to what seemed to be intractable problems.

To my teachers and guides–both human and not–who have taught me so much as well as "Mother Westward" who gave rise to my planetary perspective.

To David for taking me on the journey of writing this book.

And lastly, to those who are, and those who will be, part of the crew on TSE.

Tim

Contents
This Spaceship Earth

Acknowledgements..i

Introduction..iii

CHAPTER 1: This Spaceship Earth.................................1

CHAPTER 2: The Quartermaster's Report.....................7

CHAPTER 3: How Did We Get Here?..........................19

CHAPTER 4: Some Perspective...................................35

CHAPTER 5: Forgive and Face Forward.....................47

CHAPTER 6: The Earth Century.................................57

CHAPTER 7: Resident CO_2: We are a 730 Species,
Living in a 1230 World...........................69

CHAPTER 8: Things Humanity Can Do and the Urgent Need
to Do Them..81

CHAPTER 9: What Can I Do?....................................105

CHAPTER 10: Metamorphosis and a Call to Action....................121

References..127

Biographies..145

Acknowledgements

We would like to thank all those thinkers, visionaries, and astronauts who have helped to create the clear image of Spaceship Earth: R. Buckminster Fuller, Marshall McLuhan, Stewart Brand, Bill McKibben, Al Gore, Rachel Carson, David Orr, Chris Jordan, Jane Goodall, David Crane, Edna Lawrence, John Todd, Vandana Shiva, Wes Jackson, Janine M. Benyus, David Suzuki, Mathis Wackernagel, Pliny Fisk III, Rocky Mountain Institute, Bill Mollison, Lynne Hull, James Lovelock, Betsy Damon, Buster Simpson, Peter Stebbing, Josephine Green, Ezio Manzini, Rachel Cooper, Maurille Lariviere, Raimo Nikkanen, R. Stuart MacKay, 'Katy' Payne, Thomas Kunz, Kysa Johnson, Aldo Leopold, Maude Barlow, Ed Chiles, and Sylvia Earle.

We would like to thank all our friends, colleagues, students and staff at the Ringling College of Art + Design who have continually helped to create a vibrant and stimulating place to collaborate and grow. A particular thanks to President Larry Thompson whose leadership and vision have helped create an environment where creativity can grow and thrive. Thank you to Doug Chismar, who introduced the authors to each other, and who has been an intellectual stimulant to both of us.

Thank you to Melissa Baron and her enterprise Visionairium for the steadfast editing of this book, and to Rod Eterovic and his company Coliphics for the professional formatting. They made the book better and easier to read. Thank you to Dave Abrahamsen and his What2Design firm for the design of the cover and the companion website www.thisspaceshipearth.org. Thanks to Devin Lee Ostertag for supporting us as needed to launch the web site, and the YouTube channel that supports and expands upon the book.

All of the people named on this page helped in some way in the creation of this book. Thank you!

Introduction

There is a developing urgency around humanity's relationship to Earth. What had been speculation has now become fact. What had been theorized, is now being experienced. Climate change, super storms, highly unusual weather, historic droughts, floods, and sea level rise make us realize that this is not the planet or biosphere we used to know.

Is humanity at risk? Is humanity at cause?

Well, yes and yes.

David and Tim met in a classroom. David had become Futurist in Residence and Guest Lecturer at the Ringling College of Art + Design where Tim had been a long-time Professor of Environmental Studies. Once David started to guest lecture in Tim's classes, a friendship began, which then led to the creation of this book as an on-going, deep, and wide-ranging discussion of humanity's relationship with its planetary home.

Early in his career as a futurist, David had developed a reputation for writing and speaking about the energy landscape, correctly forecasting the explosive increase in the price of oil on the one-hand, and the soon-to-occur rapid growth of the alternative energy on the other. He authored and co-authored six books, two of which contained writings on these topics. In the latter, he wrote about the need for humanity to move to a global systems view of energy. It was this view that he brought into Tim's classroom.

Tim has spent a lifetime looking at all aspects of nature, energy, and humanity's relationship with the planet. Through a variety of jobs, teachings, writings, studies, and engagements, Tim developed an understanding of the need to reconnect human activity and the built environment with ecological systems, as well as some clear insights as to how that might be done. Among the early aha moments, the realization that science and technology, in and of themselves, evolved and were not the answer—those fields of study needed to be combined with art and design to achieve both the pragmatic and poetic solutions humanity would need. The other key component of moving forward was that telling people what to do was not a path to change, harmony, or commitment.

Change is a *will-you* question, not a *can-you* question. Change requires some degree of an emotional commitment. There needs to be a real or implied invitation, and for most there needs to be a discernible pathway with some type of reward along the way. The reward cannot be at the end, because everything is in process; we live in a world of change.

Although David and Tim took very different paths to arrive at this friendship and collaboration, they do share common ground, and much of it centers on 'the question.' Whatever the topic is, the critical issue is—are we (collaboratively speaking) asking the right question. Is it the right question? Is the question significant enough to truly allow a solution that is viable, adaptable, functional, long-term? Most importantly, is humanity facing the future when seeking the answer?

As an example, Tim was sitting on a committee, when this question was posed—what is the best light bulb to use in the new classroom? (First, let us say we agree with you—only an Academic Institution would need or want a committee to answer such a question). But this is a classic case of trying to find the right answer to the wrong question. The framework of the question sets the discussion to focus on wattage of light, and the type of bulb—incandescent versus florescent versus compact florescent or LEDs. The better question would have been, how do you illuminate a teaching/learning space so that the lighting helps everyone achieve their goals over the lifetime of the classroom? Now the discussion includes the context and function of the space and can expand to windows, skylights, room lights, task lights, natural light, dynamic lighting, direct lighting, back lighting, reflected light, light shelves, shading and diming options, and more. What makes the second question the better question? The reality of the space makes it better. The room had not been built solely so it could be lit; it had been created to help students learn.

When it comes to humanity's relationship and interdependency with This Spaceship Earth, it appears that we have been trying to find the right answer to a wide range of wrong questions, small questions and poor questions. We left out the interconnectedness of things when we formed the questions. But, given the rate of population growth coupled with the increasing rate of resource demands, interconnectedness was not the ingredient to forget.

Are we willing to change the process and get the questions right and big enough—so that we can find integrated and systems-based answers that actually resolve situations, solve multiple problems, and do that in a future forward manner? Can we find the stories that encourage others to reflect and discover the intergenerational and interspecies responsibilities that we have in common? Can we find the alternative ways of doing things—and show enough of them—so that the new path that we need to take is sufficiently inviting to make it worth exploring?

We are in a changing, dynamic, planetary situation that has never existed during modern humanity's time on Earth. We are convinced that this calls for a new consciousness, a planetary crew consciousness. We reach this new level of awareness through a process. First, we take stock of the status of our planetary spaceship. Next, we forgive what has happened, as we all played a part in what has taken place. We then let go of past models of thought and implementation. Lastly, we face forward, think differently, and (re)discover smarter and more elegant ways to interact with and operate This Spaceship Earth. Soon!

Chapter 1

THIS SPACESHIP EARTH

Spaceship Earth

Spaceship Earth is where all humans live. There is no other known planet inhabited or inhabitable by humans, this is our only place. When viewed from space, this planetary home of ours seems a tiny beautiful blue orb in the blackness of space. It is the vessel in which we live, and upon which we can thrive.

The term Spaceship Earth, or variations of it, has been used intermittently for more than a century. It was largely R. Buckminster Fuller who made the term popular starting with his book "Operating Manual for Spaceship Earth," published in 1969. That book, along with the famous "Earthrise" photo taken December 24, 1968 by Apollo 8 mission lunar module pilot, astronaut Major William A. Anders, gave us all a true sense of how unique Earth is in the known universe. It should be a reminder of how precious Earth's health is to us.

If we all could start to think of our planet as a spaceship, we would have a shift in consciousness.

We know of spaceships from the space programs and science fiction. They are a craft of finite space and limited resources in which humans live. The crew has to be efficient as energy, water, and food are in limited supply. The craft is self sufficient only to the extent that the crew and their technology are capable of creating the next generation of resources from the remnants of past generations' used material. The individuals living on these mobile space islands need to co-exist. Any problem with or on the spacecraft is a liability for all those on board. It is collective and collaborative survival in the extreme.

Now, think of Earth as Spaceship Earth with the same language. It is inhabited by humans—billions more than when Fuller wrote his book. It has a finite amount of resources so sustainability and efficiency are increasingly important. Water and food are precious. Due to the current human population of 7.3+ billion and our growing impact on the quantity and quality of resources, humanity is experiencing their spaceship's limitations. The air that many breathe is polluted. Much of our fresh water supply is being threatened. There are many issues about the food we eat, including over 900 million of us that are undernourished.

Humans now live in ever-closer quarters and need to get along. Everyone on Earth today is down-wind or down-stream from someone else, so a problem anywhere on the planet, in some way, is a problem for all on the planet.

There is one major difference. While spaceships and space stations can be refueled and resupplied from the home planet; that is not an option for Spaceship Earth. There is no other planet in the foreseeable future that can rescue, resupply, or serve as refuge for the inhabitants of Planet Earth. The critical difference between the spacecraft of the space programs and science fiction with Spaceship Earth is simply that: we live on a spaceship that must resupply itself from itself. This is why we need to understand that we are crew not passengers.

Crew	*the group of people who operate a ship, airplane, or train*
Passenger	*a person who is traveling from one place to another in a car, bus, train, ship, airplane, etc., and who is not driving or working on it*

—Merriam Webster Dictionary

This Spaceship Earth

In this early part of the 21st century, we have now entered the time on Spaceship Earth in which the problems we face are in common and transcend political boundaries. To solve them, humanity will need to be collaborative in the extreme while thinking and acting at a planetary level. That is where we are.

As the Quartermaster's Inventory of Spaceship Earth in Chapter 2 will indicate, human beings have exploded in number in the last few decades. There are 300% more humans alive today than in 1950. Our sheer numbers and way of life are having a critical effect on all other forms of life on the planet. We are crowding out and making extinct other species at an unprecedented rate. We are experiencing profound changes in weather and sea level. The temperatures are rising. The status of the spaceship has moved into the critical area. All of this is now noticeable and documented.

We continue to live, act, and think as we have for decades, centuries, and millennia. Yet, there are too many of us to continue to maintain this path. In addition, the fundamental change of how we have lived in the last 200 years has accelerated our predicament. The Industrial Age began when there were only 1 billion people alive. At that population size, the Industrial Revolution might have been sustainable at a planetary level. It is not with 7.3+ billion people.

At this time, we are beyond equilibrium on This Spaceship Earth. A spaceship can only sustain itself if it stays within its resources and resource footprint. As of this writing, humanity is operating with a footprint of 1.6 of planetary resources. We are using 60% more planetary resources every year than can be replenished. We crossed the sustainable threshold of 1.0 about 40 years ago. What form of logic or belief can allow us to think that a continuation of this trend can result in anything other than disaster? The historical thinking of separateness, limited cause and effect, and living in conceptual and psychological silos that are unconnected has delivered us to this moment.

Yet, we fight with each other. We fight economic battles and real wars. We fight over land, water, energy, religion, race, ways of life, and boundaries. This is the story of human history. The problem is that we have populated the planet to the point where continuing that history could well lead to planetary catastrophe. We risk fighting each other to the point where all of us are at risk on a degraded, polluted, and stressed planet. At that point, we all lose.

We can think we are different from each other—and we are.

We can have different points of view—and we do.

We can be of different religious faiths—and we are.

We can stand in our differences—and we always seem to do so.

For all of our short history—in planetary terms—this sense of separateness has defined us. We will probably always need to have this sense of differentiation, though less so in the future than today. One's country, religion, race, and individuality all help to give one a sense of self that separates me from you and us from them.

But now in the early part of this century, all of our differences are being overshadowed by the reality that we are all together on Spaceship Earth. That all-inclusive reality now trumps all the separate realities we hold so dear.

We have entered the Shift Age; the age and time of transition in the evolution of human thinking and consciousness from separateness to a planetary frame of reference.

> With the global economic changes
> underway and the resultant social changes
> taking root, we are developing the identity
> of global citizens. Whether one has come to
> this new identity through one's business or
> line of work or through political or cultural
> issues, we all, to varying degrees, see
> ourselves as global citizens. Globalization
> is no longer simply an economic term: it
> is the term of what is and what will course
> through all aspects of human society
> for the twenty years of the Shift Age. We
> have entered the global stage of human
> evolution.
>
> —David Houle
>   from "Entering the Shift Age" (2013)

This is the time that humanity must rapidly move into how we view all of us on planet Earth. This is the time that future historians will look back upon and note as the time when humanity transitioned from the consciousness of the nation state to the larger planetary scale of human consciousness and evolution. The only other option is some catastrophic reversal of history.

This Spaceship Earth is the name for the specific state of the planet at the early stage of the 21st century. This Spaceship Earth (TSE) is the planet today. It is this large concept that shapes our thinking and will change our consciousness. You may be from Florida, Chicago, London, Mumbai, Shanghai, or Rio. You may be of this state or that province. You may think you are a citizen of a nation. But first and foremost, you and those places are all on Spaceship Earth. That is the one thing we all have in common—we live on the same planet, and we have no other spaceship. All we have, and all humanity will have, is TSE.

Of course, we can and will continue to see ourselves as citizens of different countries or members of different religions and groups. But all of us in these groups must now realize that we are all threatened to some degree by not first thinking of ourselves as inhabitants of This Spaceship Earth. We all live, work, and worship here and want to continue to do so. Unless we now move to a higher collective consciousness of all living on TSE, our long-term existence will be challenged by what we have been and are doing. We have been unconscious passengers on TSE. We must now move as quickly as possible to a new way of thinking of ourselves as conscious crew of TSE.

We are now in the fourth age of Modern Humanity.

- ▶ *Tools defined the Agricultural Age*
- ▶ *Machines defined the Industrial Age*
- ▶ *Technology defined the Information Age*
- ▶ *Consciousness will define the Shift Age*
  —David Houle
    from "The Shift Age" (2007)

Thinking as crew members of TSE is one of the fundamental manifestations of our change of consciousness that will then lead to a collective change in our behavior towards TSE. We all must become, first and foremost, aware and <u>active</u> crew members on This Spaceship Earth. As many of us as possible, need to move to this dramatically altered sense of self and place as soon as possible.

What our future will be and how it will unfold is dependent upon our changes in thought, action, behavior, and awareness, coupled with the speed of our transition, without relapse, to TSE consciousness.

As we will make perfectly clear in this book, as of 2015, we have already created a future that is far different from what we have experienced in the last millennium. We have already taken actions, the consequences of which will bring unprecedented change to the planet in the years and decades ahead. Trillions of dollars of losses, millions of lives lost or disrupted, tens of thousands of species lost or soon to become extinct. This will happen even if all of us developed TSE crew consciousness today. We must move to share, live, and act with this new consciousness as soon as we can. The mission and vision of this book is to accelerate the *crew* consciousness of humanity as fast as possible.

As we change from being unmindful passengers to conscious crew members of TSE, we need to inventory the status of our spacecraft and assess the implications of our needs and desires related to the quantity and quality of the resource base. We need this information to ensure that we, the crew, can interact with TSE in a way that benefits both TSE and the longevity of the crew.

Chapter 2

THE QUARTERMASTER'S REPORT

The Quartermaster supervises, stores, and distributes supplies and provisions. The Quartermaster is also the one responsible for making sure equipment, materials, and systems are available and functioning. This is not about what is preferred or desired, but what is. Therefore, in the world of the Quartermaster, if a 16 oz. glass has 8 ounces of liquid, the glass is neither half full nor half empty—it simply has 8 ounces of liquid.

The purpose of the Quartermaster's Report is to put forth the data that describes the status of the ship, in this case "This Spaceship Earth." The reason for taking a planetary perspective is to realign our individual viewpoints and assumptions about resource quantity, quality, and demand with that of TSE's current operational capability, capacity, and actual status. Inputs, throughputs, and outputs need to be in dynamic equilibrium with each other to maintain the life support systems (LSS) of TSE relative to the health of the crew.

What follows is the report on the current status of Spaceship Earth as of September 2015. Some of the data will be surprising—even alarming to the reader. It is rare for such a broad range of data sets to be presented simultaneously. In doing so, we shift the context of the information from an insular or silo frame of reference to a more holistic and planetary perspective. The data is not interpretive, it is simply factual. We have sought out the most current reports available and have used those publications to establish the Quartermaster's report. There are two questions you might consider as you read the report. First—How well do your assumptions about each topic match the reality of the data? Second—Does the information reflect an outcome that you wish humanity to achieve? Your reflection upon your answers to those two questions will determine your role in defining and creating our common future.

Note: In this book, we have used both the US unit of weight (ton) and the metric unit of weight (tonne) based on how the original data was presented in the report cited. If you wish to do the conversion of units, a metric tonne is 1000 kilograms (kg) or approximately 1.10 US tons or 2,204.6 pounds. A US ton is 2000 pounds or approximately 0.907 metric tons or 907 kilograms.

Human population ⬆ increasing (estimated to be 8 billion in 2025, and 8.7 billion in 2035)

Life support system TSE ⬇ in decline, not passively reversible

Life Support System Components:

Air quality ⬇ in decline: not passively reversible

Availability of safe, potable water ⬇ in decline, not passively reversible

Habitat quantity, quality, diversity ⬇ in decline, not passively reversible

Commercial fish stocks ⬇ in decline, not passively reversible

Population of non-human vertebrate species ⬇ decline, not passively reversible

Population of assessed plant species ⬇ in decline, not passively reversible

Rate of species loss ⬆ increasing, not passively reversible

Greenhouse gas emissions ⬆ increasing, not passively reversible

Average global temperature ⬆ increasing, not passively reversible

Sea level ⬆ rising and Rate of sea level rise ⬆ increasing (Neither are passively reversible given current trends in greenhouse gas emissions.)

Extreme weather events ⬆ increasing, not passively reversible

Waste generation ⬆ increasing, not passively reversible

Note: "not passively reversible" means that the trends can only be reversed through active engagement and continuous commitment to improve and repair the system.

Crew on board

Current human population: 7,307,492,161

Current net population/crew growth rate is 148 people per minute.

World Population milestones:

1804   1 billion

1927   2 billion

1960   3 billion

1975   4 billion

1987   5 billion

1999   6 billion

2011   7 billion

2025   8 billion—estimated

2043   9 billion—estimated

Since the first manned space flight on April 10, 1961, TSE's human/crew population has increased by 233%.

The status of the human crew:

Status	Population
Illiteracy	122 million youth crew members
Lacking minimum literacy skills	775 million adult crew members
Chronically undernourished	805 million crew members
Overweight	1.3 billion crew members
Obese	600 million crew members 18 and older
Overweight or obese	42 million crew members age 5 or younger
No access to clean water	783 million crew members
Not enough access to clean water for adequate sanitation	2.5 billion crew members
No access to safe and affordable surgery	4.8 billion crew members
Asthma	334 million crew members
No access to electricity	1.3 billion crew members
Rely on the use of biomass for cooking	2.7 billion crew members

Status of the life support system of TSE

Air quality

- 1 in 8 global deaths is attributable to air pollution exposure.
- Air pollution is considered the largest single environmental health risk.
- More people die from air pollution exposure than die from lung, liver, stomach, bowel, breast, esophageal, pancreatic, prostrate, and cervical cancers combined.
- Air pollution kills more people than a combination of smoking, diabetes, and road deaths.
- Air pollution was also linked to low birth weight in babies, miscarriages, pediatric cancer, asthma attacks, and reduced fertility in both males and females.

Water availability

- The total volume of water of Earth/TSE is estimated at 1.386 billion km³ (333 million cubic miles), with 97.5% being salt water and 2.5% being fresh water.
- Of the fresh water, only 0.3% is in liquid form on the surface.
- Of the liquid surface fresh water, 87% is contained in lakes, 11% in swamps, and only 2% in rivers.
- Water is increasingly in short supply due to growing demands from agriculture, an expanding population, energy production, and Climate Change.
- A billion people on TSE lack access to safe drinking water.
- 700 million people suffer today from water scarcity.
- 2.7 billion find water scarce for at least one month of the year.
- Agriculture uses 70% of the world's/TSE's accessible freshwater.

The total volume of water of Earth/TSE has not changed while there has been life on TSE. The amount of water is the same as it was 1 million years ago.

Water quality

- Unsafe or inadequate water, sanitation, and hygiene cause approximately 3.1% of all deaths worldwide.
- Unsafe water generates 4 billion cases of diarrhea per year resulting in 2,200,000 deaths per year—mostly in children under the age of 5.
- Every day, 2 million tons of sewage and other effluents drain into the world's waters.

We add 800,000,000,000,000 plastic microbeads to the wastewater treatment system everyday in the USA. An estimated 8 trillion of those microbeads are discharged into aquatic environments daily. The remainder of the microbeads are trapped in the solids or sludge of the settling tanks and may re-enter the environment depending upon how the solids and sludge are processed.

Every year, more people die from unsafe water than from all forms of violence, including war.

Aquatic and marine environments

- Marine vertebrate populations have declined by 49% between 1970 and 2012.
- Tropical Reefs have lost more than half their reef-building corals over the last 30 years.
- Globally, there are 405 dead zones (places with too little oxygen to support marine life) in coastal waters. Collectively, they comprise an area of 95,000 square miles and the number of dead zones increased by 33% between 1995 and 2007.

In 1997, Charles Moore discovered a region of the Pacific Ocean with a large amount of plastic debris. This area is commonly referred to as the Great Pacific Garbage Patch (GPGP). While the gyre resulting from ocean currents defines the location of the garbage patch, it is land-based plastics and marine debris that constitute the make-up of the GPGP. Plastics do not biodegrade but physically break down into smaller and smaller pieces over an extended period of time. The slow rate of mechanical break down of plastics combined with the high volume of use of plastics results in the growing dimension of the GPGP. Subsequent to the discovery of the GPGP, 4 other garbage patches have been found—one in each ocean. In 2013, UNESCO symbolically recognized the Garbage Patch Nation comprised of the 5 areas of concentrated discarded material—one in each major gyre of the North Pacific, the South Pacific, the North Atlantic, the South Atlantic, and the Indian Ocean. At the time of recognition, the population of the Garbage Patch Nation consisted of an estimated 36,939 tons of garbage and covered an area of 15, 915,933 square miles. It is estimated that 80% of the population is from land-based sources.

Food supply

Fish stocks

- Overexploited/depleted stocks are at 30% (up from 10% in 1974).
- Fully exploited fish stocks are at 57% (up from 51% in 1974).
- Non-fully exploited fish stocks are at 13% (down from 40% in 1974).
- Populations of the fish family that include tuna, mackerel, and bonito, have fallen by almost 75% since 1970.

Live stock population

- 19 billion chickens
- 4.5 billion cattle, sheep, goats, and pigs

Land use

- Humans have modified more than 50% of the Earth's land surface.
- 26% of TSE's ice-free land is used for livestock grazing.
- 33% of the croplands on TSE are used for livestock feed production.
- Current loss of arable land is 46,332 sq. miles/yr (12,000,000 hectares/year) due to drought and desertification. This rate is 30–35 times the historical rate.
- Half of the topsoil on TSE has been lost in the last 150 years.
- Rate of deforestation: 46,000-58,000 square miles per year (11–15 million hectares/yr).

Climate

The 2012 estimate for global anthropogenic CO_2 emissions was 34,500,000,000 tonnes, which is the equivalent of launching **273 elephants/sec** into the air for an entire year—assuming an average elephant body weight of 4 tonnes.

Since the industrial revolution:

- Atmospheric CO_2 has risen from 280 ppm to 401.52 ppm (31 March 2015). The increase in CO_2 has not been linear.
- From 1850 to 1950, CO_2 levels rose from 288ppm to 315 ppm, an increase of 27 ppm over 100 years.
- From 1950 to 2015, CO_2 levels have risen from 315 ppm to 401 ppm, an increase of 86ppm in 65 years.
- In 1950, CO_2 emissions were just over 6 billion tonnes per year.
- Now CO_2 emissions are 34.5 billion tonnes per year.

The current atmospheric CO_2 levels are the highest they have been in 800,000 years. Homo sapiens have been on TSE for 200,000 years.

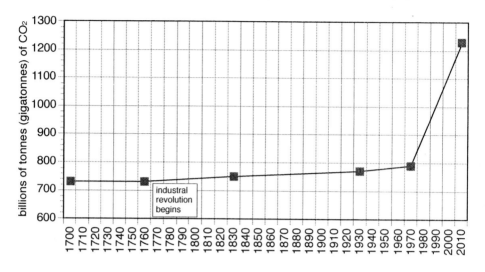

Resident CO2 In The Atmosphere From 1700 To 2010

Sea level

- Prior to 1900, sea level in the modern era had been relatively constant.
- From 1900 to 1990, tide gauge data indicates that sea level was rising at approximately 0.047 inches per year (1.2 mm per year).
- From 1990 to 2010, sea level rose at a rate of 0.12 inches per year (3mm per year) or 2.5 times faster than it had in the previous 90 years.
- The Global Mean Sea Level has risen 4 to 8 inches since 1900.

Average global temperature

- The average global temperature in 2014 was 58.42 F (14.68C), which was 1.22 F (0.68 C) above a 1951–1980 average.
- 2014 marked the 38th straight year in which the global average temperatures were above the 20th century average.
- May, June, August, September, October, and December of 2014 were all the warmest months on record, globally.
- The amount of warming is not uniform across the planet, with the greatest warming occurring between 40N and 70N Latitude.

Species

- The population of non-human vertebrate species has declined by 52% since 1970.
- Currently, 25% of all mammal species, 12.5% of all bird species, 33% of all amphibian species, and 70% of all assessed plant species are considered threatened or endangered.

Waste

- 1,300,000,000 tons of the food produced for human consumption is lost and/or wasted every year. That is approximately 1/3 of the food produced.
- Approximately 1/3 of the worldwide fisheries catch of 93 million tons is wasted—thrown back into the sea dead or dying. This bycatch is not included in the above data.
- Globally, we generate 1,300,000,000 tonnes of municipal solid waste per year.
- The average American throws out 5 pounds of trash per day.
- 500 pounds of non-biodegradable plastic enters the marine ecosystem every second.
- Over 58% of the total amount of energy produced in the United States from all sources is lost before reaching the appliance.

The increase in pollution coupled with the degradation of resources is an indication that TSE is currently being operated outside its margins of safety.

At present, humanity is operating TSE at a level that would require 1.6 TSEs to balance both the consumption of resources and the generation of pollutants with TSE's bio-capacity to generate useful biological material and absorb waste. Humanity has pushed TSE 60% over the red line, and the overshoot is increasing.

Humanity's ecological footprint

The number of Planet Earths we need to meet our demand for renewable resources and absorption of our waste is measured by ecological footprint.

Year	Humanity's Global Footprint
1961	0.75
1965	0.82
1970	*1.00*
1975	1.10
1980	1.15
1985	1.14
1990	1.22
1995	1.25
2000	1.30
2005	1.46
2010	1.50
2015	1.56

Humanity's ecological footprint was first calculated in 1961. At that time, humanity operated in a manner that maintained a surplus of resources. By 1970, humanity was in a break-even model of demand for resources relative to the regeneration of resources. Unfortunately, in the early 1970s, we crossed the line and ever since have been operating with a growing deficit. It now takes the capacity of more than one Planet Earth to meet our demands and neutralize our waste.

Since 1961, humanity's ecological footprint has more than doubled, increasing from 0.7 planets/TSEs to 1.6 planets/TSEs. The largest change has been in the carbon footprint, which has increased from 36% of the footprint to 53%. In 2014, Earth Overshoot Day was August 19th. Earth Overshoot Day is the date on which humanity consumption of resources exceeds TSE's capacity to regenerate those resources in a year.

Year	Overshoot Date
1987	December 19
1990	December 7
1995	November 21
2000	November 1
2005	October 20
2010	August 21
2014	August 19
2015	August 13

The Quartermaster's Report is a current snapshot of humanity's interaction with TSE. The report is numerically factual. Readers and users of the report can interpret the information for themselves, with the proviso that their review includes the full data set not just selective parts.

In reviewing the Quartermaster's Report, the authors feel that several questions come to the forefront.

- Did the crew know this was the status of TSE?
- Is this what the crew wanted the status of TSE to be?
- How did this become the status of TSE?
- And finally, how can the crew operate TSE to insure the vitality and viability of the LSS (life support system) for the intended journey into the future?

Chapter 3

HOW DID WE GET HERE?

*Some people don't like change, but you
need to embrace change if the alternative
is disaster.*

—Elon Musk

The September 2015 Quartermaster's Report shows that we have not
been sufficiently engaged in serving the ship upon which we live and
are dependent. We have enjoyed the harvesting of resources without
considering the long-term effects. We have modeled our actions on
the premise of an either/or mindset on a spaceship whose operating
manual is based on and/both interdependency.

*The major problems in the world are the
result of the difference between how nature
works and the way people think.*

—Gregory Bateson

Whether the future is our fate, or ours to make, is currently being decided
by the synergy of the cumulative, collective, and continuous actions that
we take. There is a planetary reaction to everything we do—it just has a
lag time before we become aware of what we have done. Too frequently,
we have chosen the gap between cause and effect as a rationale to deny
responsibility for either side of the equation. That is an option we no
longer have.

We have forgotten that the infinity of TSE is not based on a cornucopia
of resources, but on the balanced reuse of the finite governed by layer
upon layer of interactions and exchanges.

How did this happen?

Slowly, at least at first, it was done without forethought, without intent,
and without malice. No singular great event brought us to our current
relationship with the planet. We did as our forbearers did; we lived our
lives. We lived them individually, while we strove for progress and

prosperity. Primarily we were trying to do good as we defined it. Good for ourselves, our family, our tribe or clan, our country, our beliefs, our jobs or companies. And, we did so cumulatively, collectively, and continuously.

The important thing is not to stop
questioning. Curiosity has its own reason
for existing.

—Albert Einstein

Why did we get here?

As small children, we often asked the question why. Why is the sky blue? Why does the sun go away at night? Why does it rain? That curiosity is seen as endearing for a while. However, later the question loses its charm—it becomes irritating or bothersome or falls upon deaf ears. The reward, or the path of least annoyance, is to stop asking why and outwardly simply accept that which we see. We may have questions, but frequently we accept that it is better to internalize rather than voice them. We are then on the path to our present reality.

We have stopped asking why, how, who, what, where, and when. We operate on outdated and/or unverified assumptions. We are encouraged to focus our interests, to specialize, become a specific entity, and to master something. This noble pursuit also tends to promote a disconnection with other aspects of life. We are taught the value of narrowing the discussion so that we can get to a yes/no—right/wrong decision model.

The key point is that we have been taught in a model that supports and fosters isolated/siloed thinking—just focus on the subject or immediate tasks at hand. Anything outside the focal area is extraneous, irrelevant, unimportant, and nothing you need to think or worry about. It is somebody else's problem. We have been taught to support the disconnect. Curiosity is good, relative to your area of focus, otherwise it kills cats and gets in the way of finishing the job.

Do we know the consequences of our actions?

The combination of silo thinking and restricted inquiry can lead to a range of consequences. We might wish to consider them unintended or unforeseen, but they truly are consequences all the same. Washing one's face with products that contain plastic microbeads is now seen as a growing concern to marine ecosystems. The microbeads rinse off and pass through wastewater treatment systems. Given their small size, they can be ingested, but not digested, allowing the microbeads to accumulate in the fish and starve corals.

We no longer ask ourselves, "Then, what happens?" Worse, we no longer feel responsibility for what happens. Like the trash we put out by the curb—things just go away. On TSE, there is 'no away.' The plastic microbeads do not disappear just because our face is clean. They go somewhere and do something. In this case, the *doing something* is putting another life form at risk. The same is true with trash. TSE does not get lighter because the trash went away; it is somewhere. We like the convenience of out of sight, out of mind. However, just moving stuff around is not a functional or beneficial TSE solution. Ignorance regarding somewhere and something is not bliss, but a liability.

> *It is difficult to get a man to understand*
> *something when his salary depends upon*
> *his not understanding it.*
> —Upton Sinclair

MOOP—matter out of place—is a loss of potential resources and a drag on the Life Support System—LSS of TSE. The difficulty is that we assumed the bounty of the planet was always going to be available to us. The sea was so bountiful that we could not possibly overfish it. The forests were so vast, the little bit that we harvested would never be missed. The soil was so fertile, there would always be crops. Game animals were so prevalent, there would always be food. Given this abundance, what did we do? We caught fish, cut forests, farmed, grazed the landscape, and built homes, cities, and industries.

Absence of malice

No one was doing any of those things to cause harm. They were trying their best to better their lives and promote the economic viability of their community. They were focused. They were utilizing their education and circumstances. They were living their beliefs. That education and those beliefs both assumed that the model of disconnect was right—

all things in isolation. Breaking processes down into small steps and perfecting those to maximize efficiency and effectiveness of that particular operation was considered the best practice. Pollution was the cost of doing business. Economic models supported the utilization of externalities to enhance profits. The common belief was the solution to pollution was dilution. The thinking was - the planet is so big how could the byproducts and waste products of a single business or development ever be enough to cause harm, fill the air, or damage water quality? After all, the rationale for doing this was for the sake of the greater good—to provide a better life for our customers and stockholders.

Getting the metaphor wrong

Unfortunately, the issue was not what we thought it was. The issue was not immediate availability, but context. Could we harvest resources in a manner commensurate with their renewability? That was the forgotten, unasked, or unanswered question of late 20th century development.

For most of human existence, our population has been too small and dispersed to alter significantly, or permanently, the LSS of TSE. Consequently, the question of harvest relative to renewability was dealt with at a local level not the species level. We never developed a planetary perspective. There have been precautionary tales of civilizations that collapsed when either they got out of balance with their environment, or their environment went through a phase of dramatic change. But, those have been generally viewed as exceptions to the rule of progress.

However, as our population, demand for resources, and the production of commodities grew, we pushed the envelope—until the late 1980s, when we crossed the point of equilibrium with TSE.

> *Human beings are good at many things,*
> *but thinking about our species as a whole*
> *is not one of our strong points.*
> —David Attenborough

Cumulative, collective, and continuous

In many ways, we, as humans, behave and act as all species do.

- We need to use resources.
- We need food.
- We need water.
- We seek/build shelter.
- We inhale and exhale.
- We generate biological waste.

We interact with the environment, as do other living organisms, and as we do, we change the environment. We differ from other species in two significant ways. First, we are an everywhere species. Second, we have the capability to understand the effects of what we do. By everywhere, we mean just that. There is no part of the biosphere, atmosphere, lithosphere, or hydrosphere that we do not use or impact. No other single species has ever had that capacity.

To understand our impact—we can and do measure water quality, air quality, economic throughput, population numbers, and a variety of other health and environmental indices. After all, we cannot use information that we do not have, nor can we understand the value of the answer to the unasked question. However, having the information and using the information are two separate and distinct activities.

While the problems we currently face on TSE look big and can seem insurmountable, we must remember that none of them started out that way. A single car did not cause smog in Los Angeles. A single smokestack did not cause acid rain. One leaking refrigerator or one air conditioning unit did not cause ozone depletion. A single entity did not cause water pollution. The discussion and concerns of over population was not triggered by one birth. Species loss was not the fault of a single grocery store restocking of shelves. A single power plant did not cause CO_2 levels to rise. And, it was not just one city, or farm or housing development that was responsible for the current level of habitat loss.

We all played a part in that process. We did it together, over time, and still engage in the activities that expand and exacerbate the issues. If our cumulative, collective, and continuous interactions were the underlying cause, then the combination of our individual efforts to resolve the problems can have the scale of beneficial results. We do not live in a world based on isolation. Consequently, what we do, matters. In our daily choices, we make things better or we make things worse. We are crew on This Spaceship Earth, not passengers on the non-existent Cruise Ship Earth.

> *Our identity includes our natural world,*
> *how we move through it, how we interact*
> *with it and how it sustains us.*

—David Suzuki

Paradigms and perceptions

How we see, think, sense, and sort information and various sensory/ cognitive inputs is crucial to how we live our lives. Relative to perception, what is the information we are physiologically capable of taking in? Do we truly consider that while we can perceive many things, we cannot perceive everything? We see in the visual spectrum of light, but not in the realm of ultraviolet like bees, nor can we detect infrared like some snakes. We cannot hear in the low tones of Blue Whales or the high notes of echo-locating bats, nor can we hear with the speed of echo-locating dolphins. We detect a multitude of different smells, but lack the sensitivity of rescue dogs. If envy is a trait that extends beyond the human, then probably other species are impressed and desirous of our dexterity and our cognitive capability. At times, we are so impressed with what we can do, that we forget about the things we cannot. We frequently downplay the other side of the equation. Out of sight, really is out of mind. The same goes for mindsets—our paradigms.

How we organize and value information is central to our ability to promote and ensure a vibrant future for our children and grandchildren—and they to theirs. We are in constant interplay with assumptions, presumptions, what we know, what we believe, what we think, how we think, new information, missing information, how the world works, and how we wished the world worked, as well as how all those factors interact over time and at various scales. Our actions are the manifestations of our beliefs. Are we plunderers of, or partners with, TSE?

Valuing nature and nature's services

What is a stroll along the beach, or a hike in the mountains worth to you? What is the value of being able to fish along a stream or from a pier? The questions are not just about the economic value, but also the social, psychological, and physiological value. Hospital patients who have a view of green space are reported to heal as much as two days faster after major surgery. Employers report that individuals with views of natural or naturalistic spaces are more productive. Psychologists report that individuals with access to parks and green areas have less stress. There is even the *biophilia hypothesis* put forth by E. O. Wilson that people subconsciously seek connections with other species and the rest of life.

Many people consider intact ecosystems and the services they provide to be inherently valuable, even priceless, and irreplaceable. We are dependent upon nature for water, timber, fiber, as well as regulating climate, creating soil, and providing pollinators for crops. Nature is essential to the health and growth of economies, societies, and individuals.

Yet, for all of its intrinsic value, we have historically overlooked and undervalued its monetary worth when discussing business. We see nature as a thing to be removed, improved, or ignored. Rather than recognizing it as natural capital, it becomes an externality, and a repository for environmental debt. A debt that will cost other individuals or entities real money when they either have to suffer the consequences of pollution and disrupted habitats, or have to pay to restore the environment.

There are few clearer examples of our education, paradigms, beliefs, and actions being in conflict with how our planet operates than our ability to acknowledge and promote a global economy while still believing in and codifying an insular and isolated ecology. We all live down-wind, down-stream, and down-time from everybody else. We need to think, design, and operate in a systems model—a holistic context of dynamic equilibrium.

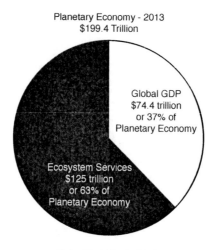

Planetary Economy - 2013
$199.4 Trillion

Global GDP
$74.4 trillion
or 37% of
Planetary Economy

Ecosystem Services
$125 trillion
or 63% of
Planetary Economy

Data: World Bank, 2013

If capitalism itself doesn't take into
account natural capital, then we're all
stuffed.

—HRH The Prince of Wales

We still have not developed a planetary perspective. We talk about a global economy, but not a planetary economy. In 2013, the World Bank estimated the global economy was 74.4 trillion dollars—the sum total of every country's GDP. They also stated that the economic value of ecosystem services was $125 trillion—or put another way—the planetary economy (Total GDP + Ecosystem Services) had a value of $199.4 trillion. So for all the tracking and concern over the trends and value of the Nasdaq, the Dow Jones Industrial Average, the Nikkei, the SSE Composite Index, the DAX and the FTSE, remember that 63% of the Planet's Economic worth is missing from all of those market indicators. Therefore, this value is disregarded when trying to improve the economy or insure the viability of the life support system of TSE.

We assume things and thus consume things. In the developed world, we have grown accustomed to having water flow from the tap any and every time we turn it on. We have grown accustomed to food being readily available via grocery stores, restaurants, and delivery services. We assume an inexhaustible supply of resources and commodities while consuming them at an extravagant rate. And seldom, if ever, question the mechanism of its availability—until now. In the U.S., California is reminding us of the flawed assumption that turning a desert into an agriculture hub for more than half of the country's fruit, nuts, and vegetables is not a viable long-term rational decision. Why? California is now in its fourth year of drought. Should we really be surprised that a desert could run short of water? A preliminary report estimates the current agricultural losses in California, because of the drought, are $2.7 billion for 2015.

Italy's olive oil industry is facing financial losses in its agricultural sector for the opposite environmental problem. The price of olive oil is rising because unusually heavy rains have set the stage for olive tree leprosy and fruit-fly blight, thus reducing the olive crop. Given that Italy is the number one country in the consumption of olive oil and is the number two country in the production of olive oil, depleting product availability will ultimately cause a shift in Italy's economic sector. Olive oil is a major crop generating approximately 3 billion euros in annual sales.

Ecologies and Economies are inexorably linked. Still in doubt, just ask the Royal Family. The bees of the UK contribute £651 million to the UK economy a year. That is £150 million more than the Royal Family brings in through tourism.

> *We see in the light of accumulated experiences, stored information, private interests and entrenched beliefs.*
>
> —George Nelson

A planetary perspective

This is why we need to develop a planetary view and consciousness. There are aspects of our assumptions and perceptions that are at odds with how TSE actually operates. As we sit at our desks writing this book, and as many of you sit in a comfortable place reading this book, our perception of movement tells us that we are being still, that we are not in motion. Yet, from a planetary perspective, when sitting still in Sarasota, Florida, one is actually spinning, rotating with the Earth, at just over 920 mph and orbiting the sun at approximately 67,000 mph. Our perception does not match our reality. And, while the local paper publishes the time of sunrise and sunset everyday, so that one can enjoy those spectacular events, we have never seen either. What we really are seeing is Earth spin, not sun rise or sun set. We orbit the sun, but our daily language perpetuates a perceptual myth that ended with Copernicus centuries ago.

There is a difference between how the planet works, and how we want/ wish the planet to work. We are a goal directed species on a process-oriented planet. Our operational preference is for linear and disconnected procedures on a planet dependent upon cyclical interconnectedness. We think and act, on the whole, in the context of the present on a planet that operates on a time scape from nano-seconds to billions of years. We believe in the concept of infinite growth relative to human endeavors on a planet of finite resources. Overcoming and/or realigning our mindsets are the key issues in coming into balance with TSE.

> *When we try to pick out anything by itself,*
> *we find it hitched to everything else in the*
> *Universe.*

—John Muir

Our pursuit of progress has been largely defined as conquering nature and improving the efficiency of products and processes. We have reshaped the land and changed the course of rivers to suit our purposes. We have been a very inventive species, but the question before us is, "Are we going to be a responsible species?"

Educationally, we have been trained to take complex problems and break them down into smaller, more understandable and comprehensible units. We tend to assume that once we know how the individual pieces work that we will know how the whole system functions, should we reassemble it. In reality, what we have deciphered is how the specific units function in isolation, while we need to know about the integration, interaction, and interplay of all the parts. We apply a reductionist framework to a holistic/synergistic planet. We have favored siloed thinking over systems reasoning. We have fostered a disconnect between TSE and ourselves.

Seeking harmony

As a child, we are taught that trees breathe in CO_2 and breathe out Oxygen, and that we, as humans, breathe in Oxygen and breathe out

CO_2. As a child, the need and the balance between trees and people is clear and real. As we get older, we are taught how to quantify the photosynthetic process—the numbers, and the equations make the process more scientific, more mechanical and more objective. The tree becomes an air handling system, analogous to those in our homes, schools, and workplaces.

As we mature, we learn the economic value of trees in board feet or reams of paper. Our education is officially complete; the tree has gone from partner to product, a product whose sole function is to serve us. It is not until we want to go for a walk in the woods or want to have a picnic in the shade that we realize what our education was lacking.

We learned to value a straight and narrow process in a world of multi-tiered interactions. We came to act as if we were apart from nature, not a part of nature. And, therein lies the rub.

We live in an economy of products dependent upon an ecology of resources. On a daily basis, it can be very easy to miss our reliance on TSE. We go to stores, but see no indication of the resources it takes to fill the shelves. Many of us routinely go to the grocery store, but seldom see a farm. We go to gas stations, but rarely, if ever, do we have any direct interaction with oil wells and refineries. And yet, many are willing to drive their vehicles to sites where they can protest oil spills. At times, even irony is invisible to us.

All businesses are dependent upon natural resources. They all use some combination of air, water, energy, raw materials, and/or refined, processed natural resources. A simple and direct translation of this reality is that the only way to have a viable long-term economy is to have a healthy long-term ecology. A corollary would be that the only way to have a long-term ecology is to have sufficient quality of life, so that ecosystems are not over stressed or harmed by humanity struggling to survive. This is something that both economists and environmentalists need to keep in mind and truly take to heart. It has never been economy or ecology; it has always been both—together. It is a dynamic interaction and exchange, but one that needs to be balanced with the reality of a One Planet System.

> *Do not limit your children to your own*
> *learning, for they are born in another time.*
> —Rabindranath Tagore

Our view, from the silo, tends to numb us to the scale of change as well as blind us to the propelling rate of change. In 1950, the world population was 2.5 billion people, of which 750 million lived in cities. We were primarily a rural world in terms of human population. Today, the world's urban population is 3.9 billion people. There are 1.35 billion more people living in urban areas today than were alive on the planet in 1950. By 2030, the urban population will be 5.04 billion people or 1.14 billion more urbanites than today—and twice the population of the planet in 1950.

In 1950, 30% of the population was urban. We crossed the 50/50 line in 2008. Today, 54% of the world's population is urban, and by 2030, it will be 60%. If we just think numbers, we will miss the implications, and therefore be unprepared for the impacts of the shift in population distribution.

You cannot meet the needs of 8.4 billion people, most of whom are urban based, using a manufacturing, economic, production, political, consumption-based, and entity-focused mindset that was developed in a time of 2.5 billion people, most of whom lived in the country. These are not those times.

To solve by design

> *We drive into the future using only our rearview mirror.*
>
> —Marshall McLuhan

> *We stand at a new threshold, and the key questions of our day are those posed by the intersection of design and life itself.*
>
> —Bruce Mau

We have a habit of operating from precedent—if it worked before, let's repeat it. If we need more, then let's do multiples of what we have done. Do more of it, do it bigger, do it faster.

Those actions do not provide the solutions for these times. We are now in the situation where we need to reconceptualize the issues. We need to redesign the process because we cannot scale up our current practices to meet the change in demands. The issues of the 21st century are radically different in scale and format than those of the 20th century.

> *Anyone who believes exponential growth*
> *can go on forever in a finite world is either*
> *a madman or an economist.*
>
> —Kenneth Boulding (economist)

Not passively reversible

When we say *not passively reversible*, we mean that in the context of our current human paradigm of life and life ways. There is a growing human population, as well as an expanding demand on the resources of TSE, to meet basic human needs and to supply the materials that keep our current operational economic methodology growing. It is the intertwined nature of the exponential demand for resources, coupled with a linear process of use (resource to product to waste) that is causing the decline in the Life Support System (LSS) of TSE. As long as we remain passive consumptive passengers, the viability of LSS will lessen and our longevity on TSE will shorten.

It is not that we cannot do things; it is just that we have to do them differently. We need to become crew and be TSE smart. For humanity to prosper, we need to determine a way to simultaneously do two things: provide quality of life for the crew, and at the same time restore and enhance the LSS of TSE. There are alternatives to every economic, agricultural, architectural, industrial, manufacturing, transportation, information, and communication process that we currently use, which can meet both goals. This means we need to actively engage the alternative processes. We can no longer confuse or conflate knowing what to do, with actually doing the right thing.

We are living transitional lives in a transformational period. The issue is meeting the goals simultaneously, not separately or sequentially. There will be no cooperative support for improving LSS at the cost of increased human suffering. Nor, can fulfilling basic needs be met by disregarding the spiraling cost of continuously degrading the LSS. Our legacy to future generations is dependent upon tackling the two issues together. Otherwise, this will generate and ensure a future with a demeaning quality of life. This is Bucky Fuller's fork in the road: utopia or oblivion. We have known this was the choice for decades and we have done our best to, ignore, ridicule, and deny it. Unfortunately, the choice has only become clearer while the level of inertia has grown greater.

> *No problem can be solved from the same*
> *level of consciousness that created it.*

—Albert Einstein

One of the central benefits of being crew is that one remembers the value of taking care of the ship. Taking care of TSE restores the opportunities and provides for the quality of life we want our children and grandchildren to have. It is a legacy that follows in the ideals of leaving a place better than you found it. The question that remains is simply— are we up to the challenge that we have brought upon ourselves?

Regaining equilibrium

If the fundamental issue of regaining equilibrium between humanity and TSE is doing things differently, then how do we accomplish that task? Solutions come not from modernizing, upgrading, or improving the efficiency and effectiveness of our predominate processes and procedures, but in reconceptualizing them with a focus on connections, integration, and resource flows. As we construct the new path forward, we need to see ourselves as active participants and causal contributors in the events, not as witnesses, bystanders, or non-involved innocents looking on from some great distance.

Driving is a prime example of the mental dichotomy of perception and effect. When driving, we are going somewhere. Our thought is not, "I am burning up fuel," but that we are trying to get to—work, the market, the store, school, church, home, and family. Our thought is, "I am driving and everybody else is traffic." Yet, we are burning fuel and converting it into N_2, CO_2, CO, NO_x, SO_2, water vapor, hydrocarbons, particulates, heat energy, and mechanical energy.

There is no intent to do harm nor do we see the harm. We did not drive some place in hopes of generating someone's asthma attack. Nor, do we participate in rush hour to deprive polar bears of habitat. In our minds, we are innocent. Yet, in our actions, we are contributors. Our silos do not let us comprehend the lag-time between cause and effect.

We have focused on making driving safer—for the driver—and on making the vehicle more fuel-efficient. Yet, the scale of use for over 1.2 billion vehicles on TSE swamps the increase in efficiency. Given the general design of cars and the reliance on the internal combustion engine, there is a limit as to how much efficiency one can gain.

If you have an internal combustion engine vehicle that gets 25–30 miles per gallon, keep in mind that less than 5% of the fuel energy is being used to move you. Or, to put it in a mind shock number—of the $50.00 used to fill the tank, only $2.50 is being used to move you. Do you still think we don't need to reconceptualize and redesign transportation and communities to reduce the need and impact of our current methodology?

The fundamental idea of design is to make the world a better place.

—Bruce Mau

Chapter 4

SOME PERSPECTIVE

Galileo

The Galileo Museum in Florence, Italy, hosts a stunning mechanical device, the Ptolemaic Armillary Sphere by Antonio Santucci. It is full of gears, circles, and spirals in an orb with Earth at the center. This model of the movement of the planets is beautiful, intricate, intriguing, complex, and it is fundamentally incorrect. While the sphere provides a model for portraying the movement of the planets as seen from Earth, it reflects the intellectual premise that Earth is the center of the universe.

Galileo recognized he was caught between truth (heliocentrism—the planets revolved around the sun) and the beliefs of his faith (geocentrism—the Earth was the center of the universe). For his truth, Galileo was found "vehemently suspect of heresy," and spent the remaining nine years of his life under house arrest. He died on January 8, 1642. It would be another 193 years before the church completely ended its opposition to heliocentrism.

> *It ain't what you don't know that gets you
> into trouble. It's what you know for sure
> that just ain't so.*
> —Mark Twain

Galileo's dilemma

Climate Change is the current version of Galileo's Dilemma. Only now, the trap is between truth and business as usual. Science and faith share an increasing alliance of agreement that the issues are real and are human generated. And, therein lies the quandary—we are cause and effect as well as solution and salvation. For many of us, our daily activities do not trigger a planetary perspective. There is no equivalent to the stock market ticker for the vitality and the viability of TSE.

The gauges on the car tell us how much fuel we have left, and how many miles we have gone, but not how much CO_2 and other greenhouse gases we have released. Our food and clothing come with a price tag, but not a map or a water meter. One can read the label on a cotton shirt and learn the brand name of the designer or manufacturer. But, that does not provide any insight as to where the cotton was grown, where the cotton was processed, where the thread was made, where the sewing was done, how the sewing was done, who did the sewing, and how those who did the sewing were treated. Nor, does the label reveal the amount of water or the volume and types of pesticides used to grow the cotton for the shirt. (660 gallons of water and 1/3 of a pound of chemicals to grow the cotton needed for the T-shirt)

Our purchases are devoid of feedback loops and mechanism that would allow us to actually make informed decisions. And, our siloed thinking only amplifies the impact of the information we do not know, do not use, and do not seek. Do the clothes we wear, and the food we eat actually support our beliefs on fairness relative to how people, animals, and resources should be treated and valued? Would we be willing to work in any of the places that made our shirts—would we want our children to aspire to those employment opportunities? We are living disconnected lives on an integrated and interconnected TSE.

Save the planet

The phrase, "Save the planet" was developed as recognition that humanity has not been acting in consort with the natural flows of Earth. We thought we could save the planet by reducing our consumption through implementing massive reduce, reuse, and recycle policies. "Work to save the planet," and "Do your part to save the planet," are phrases we have heard. Of course, this helps to create Earth awareness. It also helps to make us feel a bit better about our continuing consumer centric lifestyles when we do the three R's and become aware of our carbon footprint.

The flaw is that anything we do relative to our relationship to the planet has nothing to do with saving it!

*We are not trying to save the earth—we are
not trying to save the planet.
We are trying to save ourselves from
ourselves.*

—Tim Rumage

We know what the future of the planet will be, if the accepted view of astrophysics is to be considered. The planet has been around for some 4.5 billion years and the general thinking is that it is half way through its life cycle. There has been life on this planet for 3.5 billion years. At best, life could continue to exist for another 1.75 billion years.

The ultimate fate of life on the planet is based on the life cycle of the sun. For the past 4 billion years, the sun has been relatively constant in size, brightness, and energy output. However, in another billion years, it will enter the red giant phase of its demise. At that point, it is estimated that the sun energy output will grow by 10%—a super greenhouse effect will be triggered on Earth resulting in the increase evaporation of all forms of surface water. Over the next 2.5 billion years, the sun will also grow in size eventually incorporating the orbits of Mercury and Venus. Its brightness will grow by 40%, leading to the end of all life on Earth. Regardless of what we do, that is Earth's destiny.

Of the 4.5 billion years Earth has been in existence, humans, from our most primitive forms to the current iteration of modern humanity, have been around for perhaps 2 million years. That represents only .04 % of Earth's existence. We are a miniscule part of Earth's history and existence, and the human-planetary crisis is but a sliver of time in the life of our planet.

It is anthropomorphic hubris of the greatest sort to think that humanity can save the planet. The planet was in existence long before we were, and it will be here long after humanity has passed on, whether we last another few centuries, millennia, or even another 2 million years. Consequently, it is absolutely backwards to think that we humans can "save the planet." The purpose for the crew of TSE is to save humanity. The dinosaurs came and went—and we can too.

Timeline of Planet Earth

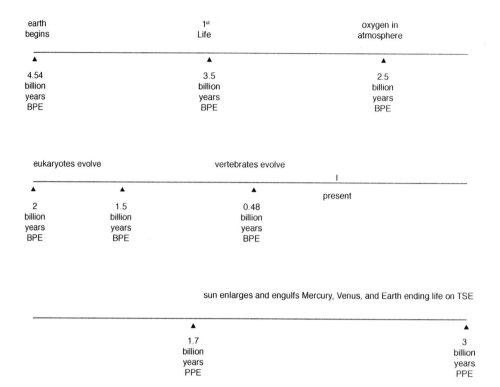

On this timeline, 1 inch is equivalent to 500,000,000 years. Using this scale, the width of the letter I (marking the present on the timeline) is approximately 17,000,000 years. Modern humans have been present for only the last 200,000 years or 0.004% of the planet's existence. The 1st life on the planet was prokaryote bacteria. Eukaryotes, organisms with DNA on chromosomes that are contained in the nucleus of the cell, evolved between 2 and 1.5 billion years BPE. (BPE means Before Present Era and PPE means Post Present Era.)

In all likelihood, we are the first and only species to know that we have a time frame of existence—and the potential ability to lengthen or shorten it. We can change the timeline by default, denial, or design. We can participate or witness our collective outcome. We can be of the spaceship or the cruise ship mindset. The future is ours to make, or the future is our fate. For the reader, the quandary you must now contend with is that your decision to engage or not, is actually a decision. You are choosing to engage or you are choosing not to engage—and that is an active choice and personal decision you have to make, and for which you are responsible. Even at this stage of this book, the age-old excuse of, "I didn't know that," has gone away. This book exists to help provide content and context, especially context so that each of us can decide where, when, and how we can become the most effective crewmember, we can be.

Moving to an operating TSE consciousness is about determining what our future will look like and how long that will be. Do we want to be around in a healthy, civilized way in the year 3,000, or do we not care? Given the pace of stress and change humanity has initiated on Earth, even that long might be far fetched.

It is not our job, nor can we, "Save the planet." We have to alter our consciousness and thinking so that we save ourselves and all the species that make up the life support system of this beautiful blue orb.

The Earth will save itself. Humanity needs to save itself. TSE is here to help us. We just have to return to, and then maintain, a relationship of dynamic equilibrium with TSE.

The Earth has been warming and cooling since Day 1

Why our conversation is about TSE, not just Planet Earth, is that TSE allows us to put relationships in the context of humanity.

Has Climate Change happened before? Yes

Has global warming happened before? Yes

Have CO_2 levels been higher before? Yes

Has sea level risen before? Yes

Have there been mass extinctions before? Yes

Have all of those trends ever reversed themselves? Yes

Then what's the issue?

The issue is that none of those things have ever happened while modern humans lived on the planet. These changes are all new to us and to our way of life. It is one thing to say that temperatures were higher in the time of the dinosaurs, but we didn't live in the time of the dinosaurs.

As the planet's environment changes, so do the species that can live on the planet. The life forms that visually dominate the Earth today are unique as they have been in each stage of the planet's development. Microbes appeared 3.5 billion years ago. Multicellular organisms, macroscopic algae, and animals have been here for 600 million years and modern humans for 200,000 years.

We are part of the 6th major crew change on TSE.

What went on before we were here?

Life and death, species coming and going, temperatures rising and falling, continents merging and breaking apart, CO_2 and Oxygen levels rising and falling, and 5 great extinction events occurred before us.

The first of the 5 great extinctions (crew changes) occurred 440 million years ago. Life on the planet was marine-based, and global cooling generated an intense ice age. Sea levels dropped 230–330 feet (70–100m) leading to the extinction of 85% (82%–88%) of all species on the planet. While most were killed during formation of the ice, there were species that died off with the melt when water with low oxygen content flowed back into the rising ocean.

After this extinction event, came the age of fishes; they became prominent in both marine and freshwater environments. During this recovery phase, the first forests developed on land and insects appeared.

The second mass extinction was 375–359 million years ago, triggered by widespread environmental changes. It is estimated that 79%–87% of all species on the planet died off. Major fish groups were killed-off, as were the corals. It would be 100 million years before coral reefs started forming again.

Yet, the die-off set the stage for the evolution of sharks, amphibians, and the great swamps of the Carboniferous Period.

The third, and what is currently regarded as the largest mass extinction event, occurred 252 million years ago. Often referred to as the "Great Dying," this event killed off 93%–97% of all species on the planet. Volcanic eruptions appeared to have been an initial trigger in the die-off. First, the sulfuric gases they emitted triggered climate cooling and acid rain, but the key factor was the even greater amount of CO_2—a heat-trapping gas— that was released by the eruptions.

The heat trapped by the CO_2 generated the highest temperature known on Earth while species have existed. The temperature of the upper ocean reached 100 °F (38 °C), and sea surface temperatures are estimated to have risen to 104 °F (40 °C), some 18–28 °F above today's average sea surface temperature around the equator. The ocean warming affected sea temperatures 10,000 feet (~3050m) below the surface, changing ocean circulation patterns, which created stratified layers of water with low oxygen content.

Photosynthesis in plants was impacted. Plants began shutting down photosynthesis at 95° F (35 °C), and plant die-offs began at 104 °F (40 °C). High latitude (polar) temperatures were 18-54 °F (10–30 °C) higher than today.

The result of the high temperatures, the lack of biological systems to take up CO_2, the die-off of plants and sea surface organisms, and the resulting changes in water, air, and weather circulation was the demise of entire ecosystems triggering cascades of species loss.

It would take 10–20 million years for the planet to regain its prior level of species diversity, but the make-up of life was very different. The dominant group of organism in this revitalization of Earth would be the dinosaurs. This was the time of vertebrates and mammal-like reptiles. It was also the time of flying reptiles, the beginning of flowering plants, and the beginning of birds.

This was followed by the fourth mass extinction event, 201 million years ago. It would kill off 76%–84% of all species. The cause of this event is poorly understood. The current research links the loss to the change in the availability of water. As sea levels dropped, species in the warm coastal areas went extinct. On land, the reduction of water led to extreme temperatures and season generating species loss and ecosystem failure. Geologically, this was a period of volcanic activity and linked to the formation of the rift zones outlining the tectonic plates.

The last of the 5 great extinctions was 66 million years ago, ending the reign of dinosaurs. Similar to the others, 71%–81% of all species died off. There is clear evidence that at east one huge asteroid impacted Earth at this time. Whether that was the causal event of the mass extinction or a contributing factor to the die-off is not as clear. The geography of Earth was significantly changing in this time. The continents were separating. Ocean currents and climate were changing. Volcanic activity was creating lava outcrops and changing the make-up of the atmosphere. Toxic gases were being released, and CO_2 was building up. The toxic gases and sulfides dropped global temperatures and yielded acid rain. Sea level dropped nearly 500 feet (150m) during this extinction event, and the acid rain killed plants impacting the ecosystems. Fewer plants supported fewer herbivores, thus supporting fewer carnivores. As the impacts of CO_2 increased, ocean acidification triggered the loss of phytoplankton and disrupted the oceanic food web. The CO_2 would also have triggered global warming increasing the temperatures by as much as 18 °F (10 °C) and warming of the oceans by 7 °F (4 °C).

Yet, this mass extinction set TSE on the path to create the crew, passengers, and partners we have on board today.

Are we, homo sapiens, the causal trigger of the 6th mass extinction event?

There is no conclusive scientific way to prove that <u>homo sapiens</u> are the causal trigger of the 6th mass extinction event, for the simple reason we have to wait for our extinction to take place before we know the answer. That would make the analysis impossible, and the results irrelevant, because it would already be too late to reverse the outcome.

But, there are some clues that might make us question the wisdom of our current activities. These clues would also promote facing the future, and designing a future we would prefer, rather than constantly trying to move forward using the past as our guide.

Looking at the first five mass extinctions, we see common threads of the impact of changing global temperatures, the impact of increasing CO_2 and greenhouse gases, the impact of habitat change, and the cascade effects that species loss can have on ecosystem make-up and viability.

Due to the combination of direct habitat changes by humans coupled with the string of secondary effects, TSE is currently losing species at 1000 times the natural background rate. Humans are generating billions of tons of CO_2 and releasing it into the atmosphere. We are already seeing average global temperature rise and acidification of the ocean.

Human activity has created 400 dead zones in the oceans—and since 1960, the number of dead zones have doubled every decade.

What each mass extinction reveals is that TSE recovers; it is life on board that is replaced. Currently, we seem to be rapidly setting the stage for our replacement crew. Is that really what we want to do? Is that what we—humanity—really means and intends to do? For unlike the previous mass extinctions, the one the planet is currently undergoing is being generated by our own activity.

We are creating ecocide.

Death by misadventure

In the British legal system, one of the options that a coroner has in listing cause of death is "Death by Misadventure." Misadventure means that the deceased was engaged in an intended action, but that action had an unintended outcome. By and large, homo sapiens do not appear to be a suicidal species, but we are clearly prone and subject to death by misadventure. We engage in many intended actions, but those actions have unintended— or ignored—consequences. Greenhouse gas emissions, as an example, are an unintended and ignored consequence of a carbon-based economy. And, Climate Change is triggering a cascade of consequences from extreme weather events, to sea level rise, social unrest, changes in agricultural, changes in ecosystems, as well as changes in human health risks.

MAD to MIS

MAD, or Mutually Assured Destruction, was a military strategy and a national security policy of the Cold War. In essence, the concept assumed that if two enemies each had a similar capability of totally destroying the other, that neither would strike first because there was no way to win.

The MAD doctrine is still with us today, but in a different form and with a different enemy. Today, the battle is within, amongst, and between ourselves. It is centered on:

*...the unresolved, unresolvable tension
in our species between selfishness and
altruism.*

—Stephen Greenblatt

Our methodology of dealing with our self-imposed MAD doctrine is to accept the status quo as the starting point, and make changes from there. This is what leads to policies of incremental change or reducing CO_2 and/or greenhouse gas emissions by X-percentage in 10 or 15 years. We put the focus on being less bad, rather than being and doing good. We ignore the fact that CO_2 and greenhouse gases are not a zero sum game or balance sheet. They all have a hang time in the atmosphere. The 35 billion tonnes of CO_2 put in the atmosphere in 2013 is still active in the environment, as is the 35 billion tonnes released in 2014. The current model of CO_2 reduction is really a lower rate of increase of CO_2 in the environment, not a true subtraction from the total. While these so called reductions are a politically and economically palatable and acceptable way to lessen the rate of increase, it still keeps us on the path of MAD.

The policy we really need is one of MIS—Mutually Insured Survival. One of the definitions of ensured survival is to make certain we take necessary measures and precautions. This is what we have to do—take necessary measures. It is not about promising that something will be done, or assuming it has been done, but about actually doing the deed.

Getting to MIS requires that we reconceptualize what the status quo should be. We need to put truth above convenience and preference. We need to support,

...the better angels of our nature.

—Abraham Lincoln

Fundamentals

As parents, we are to sacrifice for our children and not vice versa. Are we defining progress as promoting short term economic gains for a few, or is progress to be defined by increasing the viability and vitality of TSE for the future of all?

44

The earth belongs to each generation...
no generation can contract debts greater
than may be paid during the course of its
own existence.

—Thomas Jefferson

What would Jefferson think about the condition of TSE if he were alive today? Our current environmental debts will haunt the future for generations unless we actively engage in changing our behavior.

The conservation of natural resources
is the fundamental problem. Unless we
solve that problem it will avail us little to
solve all others.

—President Theodore Roosevelt

Or, to be a little more blunt,

What's the use of a fine house if you
haven't got a tolerable planet to put it on?

—H.D. Thoreau

Will we?

The issue before us is not—can we change? The issue we are facing is—will we change? Will we make the emotional commitment to our children, grandchildren, and the future to acknowledge the implications and impacts of our actions, and to solve them?

If there must be trouble, let it be in my day,
so that my child may have peace.

—Thomas Paine

The future is our fate. The future is ours to make. We have choices and opportunities. We can be shortsighted or think in terms of the long-now. It is not uncommon, at various points in our lives, to think about a five-year plan, or where we want to be in five years. Why not expand the question to things we use everyday. Where is the plastic bag you got at the store going to be in 5 years? What is the life span of plastic? If you are just using the plastic bag to get the groceries home, how will the time frame of use match the life span of the product? When we consider all the things we buy, on average only 1% of those products are still in use in 6 months. The other 99% have been trashed. Why support a system that is geared to waste a planet? Surely, there is another path to prosperity and vitality on TSE.

Agreement on change?

World leaders continuously meet to see if they can come to a binding international agreement on reducing greenhouse gas emission. Regardless of the rhetoric, what Climate Conferences are really deciding is—are we staying with MAD, or moving to MIS?

> *Our greatest responsibility is to be*
> *good ancestors.*
>
> —Jonas Salk

The biggest problem this book poses to the reader, and the user of the website www.thisspaceshipearth.org, is that now you know. All too often each of us has used the excuse that "we didn't know" something as an explanation of why we should be given a waiver on being held responsible for our actions. Now that excuse is gone. You may or may not use the information that is in this book or on the website. That is your choice. However, now you do so knowingly. It has become a conscious act on your part to either embrace or ignore your role and contribution on TSE. You have been granted all the rights and responsibilities of being crew.

Chapter 5

FORGIVE AND FACE FORWARD

Earlier, there were discussions on what we do in life, and how we each look at our lives. Primarily, we move through life from a personal perspective without any extended sense of connectivity to the whole.

We see grocery stores, but not the fields where the vegetables were grown, how the food was made, where the packaging originated, or how everything in the store arrived. We don't see the source of the energy that cools and lights the store. We don't see the end destination of the discarded packaging. And, on a very personal level, we don't know specifically where our own body wastes go, and what happens to them.

We live in perceived silos of individual lives. It is only when we scale up our thinking that the larger picture comes into view. We flush the toilet numerous times a day, getting rid of our personal waste. Now bring into perspective the 300,000 people who do the same thing in your city, the millions of people who do that every day in your state, the tens or hundreds of millions that do that in your country, or the billions of people who do that around the world–every day. Non-stop creation and disposing of human waste, every minute, hour, day, week, month, and year. Take a look at human waste from a planetary perspective. That is the beginning of thinking as an inhabitant of This Spaceship Earth.

For centuries, humans could think about life, and the cause and effect of our relationship with the world around us from an individual or family perspective. The world was so vast that the billion people who lived on it 200+ years ago could always find a new place, a place where no one was, where the air was fresh, and nature absorbed all that we gave it or left behind.

Now, as we move from 7 billion to 8 billion of us in these next few years, we have to give up the luxury of thinking this way.

We have to let go, and face forward. The world in which we lived, is gone. The legacy thinking of the past and the ways of thinking that came about when the world was a profoundly different place, must go.

It has been more than 10,000 years since the beginning of the Agricultural Age, and with it the beginnings of civilization, society and religion. Some of the foundational thinking of humanity's relationship with the world, which first came into being during this time, still prevails. We carry this foundational thinking as a filter through which we still look at the planet.

This can be seen simply in our use of words. Who among us has not used the words *sunrise* and *sunset*? These were words that came into being before Copernicus theorized, correctly, that the Earth revolves around the sun. The human perspective of living on a flat Earth, when the sun rose above the horizon and ended when it set below the other horizon, is centuries old thinking. However, we still use those words today though we know that it is the Earth that spins around the sun, and the sun is fixed. Word usage affects thoughts, and vice versa.

It is in the last 200 years that humanity, often in the name of progress, has created massive and ever accelerating change. These changes have indeed influenced our thought, but with the acceleration of human growth and consumption, our ways of thinking are rapidly becoming outdated. What occurred in the 20th century is unprecedented in terms of humanity's relationship with our planet. Developments such as the quadrupling of our population, mass production, the internal combustion engine, global use of fossil fuels, dramatically increased human life spans, plastic, and global connectivity and travel all came into being. The growth of humanity and its impact on our planet increased exponentially, yet our thinking has remained on a largely linear track. Our impact has increased and changed more than our thinking. Our thinking needs to change profoundly, and soon.

Compare the Quartermaster's Report (in Chapter Two) about the current condition of This Spaceship Earth today with what that report might have been 100 years ago.

- World Population 1915: less than 2 billion people
- World population 2015: 7.3 billion
- Number of Megacities 1915: 0
- Number of Megacities 2015: 34
  (megacities are urban areas with a population of 10,000,000 + people)

- Number of internal combustion engine vehicles:
  - *In 1915, less that 3,000,000 world wide*
  - *In 2015, over 1,200,000,000 world wide*
- Global Ecological Footprint:
  - *In 1915, less than 0.3 TSEs (estimated)*
  - *In 2015: 1.6 TSEs*
- The amount of water on the planet in 2015 is the same as 1915.

The world in which we currently live is dramatically different from the world of our parents. Our thinking and our actions need to reflect and be responsive to the different and present reality. We can look back, as long as we keep in mind that these are not those times, and that our focus and adaptation needs to be based on what is and will be, rather than what was.

> *It is easy to dodge our responsibilities,*
> *but we cannot dodge the consequences of*
> *dodging our responsibilities.*

—Josiah Charles Stamp

How?

Forgiveness.

We need to forgive ourselves for thinking the way we have, and understand that inventions occurred in a different time and without any long-term forethought. When John D. Rockefeller brought scale to the petroleum business, there were less than one-fourth of the people there are today. A new fossil fuel was not perceived at that time to be a cause of what we now know as Climate Change. It was simply a new fuel for human progress. When Henry Ford brought mass manufacturing to the automotive business, it was not clear that smog and air pollution would be a consequence. The first car in Los Angeles did not cause smog, but millions today do. When insecticides were first invented, the silo thinking that created them was to prevent human starvation. Unfortunately, silo thinking did not understand that insecticides were poisonous to the ecosystems of the world. At their inception, these inventions could not be seen as a threat to life in the way we see them today. When Einstein had the insight of $E=MC^2$, he could not have foreseen Hiroshima, Chernobyl, Three Mile Island, or Fukushima.

We are of our times. We think largely within our time, but are guided by past experiences and examples. What people thought 200 or 100 years ago must be looked at within this filter. They invented, created, and built within their time. Their time did not have air, water, and food pollution. Today we do. Their time did not have massive species extinction. Today we do. Their time was not one of living with increasingly disruptive weather patterns, and consistent increase of global temperatures. Today we do.

We must not look back and blame. We need to forgive, let go, and face the reality of today, and the crisis ahead for TSE. We need to face forward.

The concept of unlimited growth might have been a survival idea first, and then an economic concept, but it now threatens our survival. The depth to which our economic ideas from the past pervade our thought today puts us at peril.

We have to accept where we are, and what we have done. To do so, we need to let go of the blame we hold for inventions and ways of thinking that now no longer are valid.

> *If you want something new, you have to*
> *stop doing something old.*
> —Peter F. Drucker

So we start with forgiveness

We forgive

- those that unintentionally created fuels, insecticides, transportation, non-sustainable ways of consumption, and economic growth models that now are and will be creating havoc on our only place, TSE.
- those that operated solely from economic self-interest in a perceived infinite world. We forgive from the viewpoint of finiteness that we stand in today.
- ourselves for not understanding the consequences of our self-directed consumption on the planet.

- ourselves for accepting ways of thinking that now create harm to living things. Harm we did not see when we learned these thoughts.
- ourselves for pointing the finger at others as the cause of our problems. We forgive ourselves for judging others from a self-perceived perch of moral superiority.
- everyone who did whatever they did that contributed to the critical situation we are now in on TSE.
- mistakes of the past, as they were not, in most cases, mistakes made with the comprehensive whole in mind, but were purely from the developed human tendency to think, perceive, and live in silos.

Forgiveness can be granted to all of us, if we change our ways, and we let go of all the ways we have thought and acted from times when there was a fraction of our current population. Then, we didn't think, see, or understand what silo thinking might ultimately do. Nor did we think that it would lead us to the state the planet is in, as described in the Quartermaster's Report.

However, forgiving ourselves only comes if we stop our old ways of thinking and acting. Holding on to the thinking that got us to our present situation cannot be forgiven. All of the legacy thought, or lack of thinking, at the planetary level, must end for forgiveness to occur.

If ever greater numbers of us can stand in collective forgiveness, then what is next?

> *Though no one can go back and make a*
> *brand new start, anyone can start from*
> *now and make a brand new ending.*
>
> —Carl Bard

Letting go: The collapse of legacy thinking

Once we forgive, we need to let go. We need to see Legacy Thinking as a precautionary tale, of what happens when we allow silos to trump systems, and let habits or rote action preclude situational awareness. We must escape how we thought 100, 50, 25, even 10 years ago. We have to move beyond the thinking that, unknowingly, has placed us, and certainly our children and grandchildren, in peril. For, if we do not displace the legacy thinking, it will continue.

We need to let go of the thinking, "What each of us does in our daily life doesn't matter." It does.

We need to let go of the silo-based thinking instilled in us by previous models of learning and education. These are not those times. The value and/or efficiency of the part or isolated piece can no longer supersede the long view of the viability of the systems. All are interconnected and interdependent parts. Previous generations believed they didn't have to think of the whole, though we now see that it would have been a good idea if they had.

We have to let go of the ways we thought, those that brought us to the planetary status set forth in the Quartermaster's Report.

We have to let go of thinking that we can do whatever we want, and there are no significant consequences for TSE. We have to let go of politically or economically oriented ways of thinking that breed separateness and pure self-interest, at least relative to our relationship with the only home in the universe we have.

It is very difficult to let go of ways of thinking and actions,

Legacy Thinking is often why it is hard to see change, especially now because we are living in the present through the filters of the past.

Only when the change becomes personal do we understand the change. And then there is a conflict: either you have to accept that your legacy thinking is no longer valid, or you hold on for a more secure and comfortable view of the world.

> *That is why people get so upset by change—it threatens their point of view or worldview.*
>
> —David Houle
>   from "Entering the Shift Age" (2013)

Old realities are giving way to new realities. The Internet has disrupted and disintermediated almost every industry to some degree. This dynamic has changed the way we think about media, communications, retail, logistics, place, and mobility. This new global connectivity is changing how we think about work, social activities, and recreation.

The collapse of legacy thinking is now starting to happen as more and more of us think about our collective relationship with Earth. The personal experiences of very different weather patterns trigger us to think about what is going on. The general knowledge of ever increasing temperatures, and the rapid melting of glaciers and ice pack inform us that something fundamental has changed with the planet and that we are, to a great degree, at cause.

Legacy Thinking keeps us all as unaware passengers of TSE. We need to let go of thinking that what each of us does is not relevant to TSE; that is the first step to becoming crew of TSE.

Acceptance

Forgiveness is often difficult, so is acceptance. Both rely on letting go. We must let go of what got us here as well as our historic views of our relationship with TSE as these preclude us from clearly seeing the present and unfolding situations.

We need to develop acceptance that our anthropocentrically based relationship with the Planet Earth needs to change. We have been blind passengers on Spaceship Earth. Now, we need to become an aware crew of This Spaceship Earth.

As many readers must have experienced, ceasing to resist and opening up to acceptance creates new ways of seeing the world, seeing possibilities, and seeing a new self. Newness rushes in. Acceptance opens new pathways of thinking. Resistance keeps things constricted and tense. What works at the individual human level, we must now make work at the planetary level.

If we cannot accept that our relationship to TSE must change, then it will not. Every decade, year, month, week, day, and hour we postpone acceptance of what we are doing to TSE will make things ever more critical in the future. Without change, we will be perpetuating what will seem like an endless series of catastrophes.

We need to let go of the past, forgive all that was done, thought, and accept the present, and then face the future.

Face forward: Transformation

We live in a time when the speed of change has accelerated to the point that it is environmental; we live in an environment of change.

2010–2020 is the Transformation Decade.

—David Houle
from "Entering the Shift Age" (2013)

Transformation	*change in form, appearance, nature or character*

—Dictionary.com

The decade, 2010-2020, is a time when much of humanity's institutions and fundamental thinking will change. It is one of those periods in history when there is a rapid acceleration that takes humanity from what is to what will be in a very short period of time.

This book is being written in 2015, half-way chronologically through the decade. However, given that change has become environmental, we are perhaps only a third of the way through the total amount of transformation that will occur this decade. This is another way of saying that the speed of change and transformation will be twice as much during 2015–2020 as it was 2010–2015.

It is important to reflect upon this potentially exponential period. Think back on the way things were, and how you thought about them in 2010 compared to 2015. Across the board, we all think and act differently than we did five years ago. This is obviously clear in the areas of technology, media, and communications. It is also true when it comes to thinking about humanity's relationship with Planet Earth.

First decade of 21ˢᵗ century thought

Today, in 2015, there is much more awareness of Climate Change, global warming, and increasingly changing weather and extreme weather patterns than in 2010. Of course, much of that is due to the rapidly increasing evidence our planet is providing, that dramatic change is occurring. We have more evidence. That evidence has started coursing through our electronically connected human consciousness.

What was once only known locally is now known globally. We live in a warm climate, and see polar bears standing on floating ice flows. We see pictures of cities in other countries where air pollution looks like smoke. The concepts of sea level rise, scarcity of fresh water, and a warming planet are now memes that course through the electronic Neurosphere that is the collective electronic extension of human thought.

It is in this, the second decade of the 21st century, that we must change our thinking about our relationship with the only planet we have. We have to face forward. The past is gone, and so must its ways of thinking. We have to face the future, and create future facing ways of thinking and acting. When, or as, we do that, then this current decade will become known as the first decade of 21st century thought, and bring us into the Earth Century.

Chapter 6

THE EARTH CENTURY

We have entered the Earth Century. The 21ˢᵗ century is the Earth Century.

> *The twenty-first century will be the Earth*
> *Century. It will be during this century*
> *that humanity faces the reality of whether*
> *it wants to destroy itself and much of*
> *what exists on this magnificent planet or*
> *not. Assuming we make essential course*
> *corrections, future historians will write*
> *about the Earth Century as a turning point*
> *in human history.*

and

> *The Shift Age is and will be the age when*
> *humanity alters its sense in relation to our*
> *planet. This goes way beyond what we*
> *think of as the environmentalism of today.*
> *It is a much more long-term stewardship*
> *point of view. All of our previous history*
> *has been about growth, economic growth,*
> *and use of the planet's resources for our*
> *immediate needs. The Earth seemed to*
> *be unlimited in its space, resources and*
> *ability to absorb whatever humanity did.*
> *No longer.*

> —David Houle
> from "Entering the Shift Age" (2013)

This is the century when humanity will successfully move to a
TSE consciousness, or not. We have clearly entered it with *Cruise
Ship Earth* thinking, stuck in old legacy thoughts, and unable to see
beyond our specialized, silo thinking. Even as this book is written, we
collectively fail to see the cause and effect of what we are doing and the
consequences on this connected, completely inter-related planet.

Here in 2015, we are only 15% through the Earth Century. This may lead some to think, complacently, that we have 85 years to change our ways and make the move from Cruise Ship Earth ways to Spaceship Earth consciousness. This is perhaps the most dangerous thought we can hold. The complacency this way of thinking induces is in fact the enemy. We can no longer think our solutions, our gradual change of behavior, or our waiting for a big fix will save us from disaster. Legacy Thinking, with its dependence on seeing things in isolation and disconnection, blinds us to the reality of cause and effect on a TSE timeline. At least 40% of the CO_2 that humanity releases into the air today will impact the atmosphere and humanity for the next 5 generations.

As the charts later in this chapter will illustrate, we must do something significant by 2030, or we face what can only be called massively disruptive social, health, economic and ecological catastrophes for humanity.

If the goal of humanity is to live well beyond this century, then TSE has entered the Earth Century in a mission critical state. There has been no operating manual for Spaceship Earth, though Fuller suggested one was needed more than 35 years ago. His approach to a manual was thoughtful, visionary, and abstract. Now that we are in this mission's critical stage, we hope that this book, and the perspectives presented in this chapter, will begin to create a holistic operating manual of principles and practices for humanity regarding our relationship with This Spaceship Earth, based upon the realities of 2015.

The 21st Century: The Earth Century

All of our resource utilization and consumption from the dawn of man up through the 18th century was a slow linear increase. This was largely based upon slow population and commerce growth. In the 19th century, with the beginning and scaling up of the Industrial Revolution, the dramatic increase in use of fossil fuels and increasing rate of population growth, humanity's footprint accelerated.

It was in the 20th century that the reality dramatically changed. Human population quadrupled and the average per capita consumption of fossil fuels and energy soared. Consequently, these dynamics are what pushed us beyond the 1.0 planetary footprint three quarters of the way through the century.

> *In fact, we are now living in a dually
> perceived reality. While we live in the
> twenty-first century, we seem to hold- most
> people very strongly- to the "way things
> are" as what is real. Much of our daily
> lives have been habituated to this twentieth-
> century reality.... We simply accept what
> we have known all or most of our lives as
> reality...Acceptance of some-thing is, to
> some degree, acquiescence to it.*
>
> —David Houle
>   from "Entering the Shift Age" (2013)

The significance of what occurred in the 20th century needs to be changed, and quickly.

> *The issue we have today is the
> predominance of all the twentieth-century
> physical constructs that dominate the
> world.... We can't simply start anew
> with new structures, transportation
> systems, and cities, leaving what exists
> behind. There is simply no room when
> the landscape is covered with twentieth-
> century constructs.*
>
> *Simply put, for the first time in the history
> of humanity we don't have a blank canvas
> on which to paint a new picture. Painting
> and creation of the new has to be infused
> back into the old. We must develop the
> vision of the twenty-first century, then turn
> and face the landscape dealt us by the
> twentieth-century and retrofit it.*
>
> —David Houle
>   from "Entering the Shift Age" (2013)

Entering the 21st century, the vast majority of humanity has either spent most or all of their lives living in a world with a footprint greater than the planet's capacity. That is our reality, our upward sloping baseline. We have powered into this new century, operating as we have for the past 50 years. And those assumptions of 50 years ago have defined our context and perception of reality. We must now acknowledge our new and true reality—a 1.6 footprint reality.

Clearly, humanity cannot continue to live beyond the Earth's means through this century. That is why the 21st century is the Earth Century. This is the time when we must alter the trajectory, the thinking, and the practices that have placed us in this mission critical state. This is the century when humanity must create and operate in radically different ways if we want to be proactive rather than unpleasantly reactive in our species evolution on Earth.

In the early part of the Earth Century, there have been a few voices and organizations that punctured the legacy thinking of the 20th century. These started the growing awareness that we have entered a mission critical stage of TSE.

In 1988, humanity crossed the Maginot Line of Climate Change—CO_2 levels above 350ppm in the atmosphere. It was not until 2007 that we came to understand the significance of the crossing. It was Dr. James Hansen who informed us that a CO_2 level of 350ppm was the upper level of the safe zone for people and civilizations.

But, 2007 was the year of the iPhone release, the last and final volume of the Harry Potter series, the surge in Iraq, the mortgage crisis, and a break through in stem cell research. Were it not for the efforts of Bill McKibben and his students at Middlebury College, it would have been easy for the discussion of CO_2 emissions to be lost in the din of self-interest. While "An Inconvenient Truth" had ignited the conversation, it would be 350.org, founded by Bill McKibben that would be the rallying entity for continuous and growing public action on policies to reduce global emissions of CO_2. Without that foundation, it would undoubtedly take longer for TSE consciousness to take hold at a level significant enough to successfully face and shape the future.

We write this book with full acknowledgement of the powerful voices of Al Gore, Dr. Hansen, and Bill McKibben's 350.org. They have awakened the consciousness in tens of millions of people around the world with the information that we are heading for cascading catastrophes if we don't pay attention to greenhouse emissions of the past, present, and future. They have affected the thinking of the authors of this book, and we give full respect to their pioneering of what we hope will be TSE crew consciousness. It is their work in the first decade of the Earth Century that gives us hope and fortitude that we can move hundreds of millions into the consciousness of being crew of TSE, and do so in time.

However, for numerous political and economic interest reasons, people who in some way are part of the Carbon Combustion Complex have dismissed Gore, Hansen, McKibben and 350.org as alarmists, or part of some conspiracy. [President Eisenhower, America's greatest general of the 20th century famously warned America about the threat of the military industrial complex as his last message to the nation as president]. The general argument from the politicians and business people that make up the Carbon Combustion Complex is that fighting Climate Change is too costly, that it will wreak havoc to economies around the world. In this book, we have made clear that the economic costs to not aggressively face Climate Change is far greater than any perceived short term costs. We are not alone in this thinking. The most significant economic and financial minds in the world agree with us.

The World Economic Forum (WEF), held every winter at Davos, Switzerland, is generally regarded as the apex conference of global financial powers and thinkers. Every year, the organizers conclude the conference with a list of the top ten risks to the global economy. Here is what the brilliant economic minds attending the 2015 Davos conference published as the top ten risks to the global economy. The publication, "Global Risks 2015, 10th Edition," included the top 5 Global Risks in terms of Likelihood, and the top 5 Global Risks in terms of Impact.

Top 5 Global Risks In Terms Of Likelihood

	2010	2011	2012	2013	2014	2015
1st	Asset price collapse	Storms & cyclones	Severe income disparity	Severe income disparity	Income disparity	Interstate conflict with regional consequences
2nd	Slowing Chinese economy (<6%)	Flooding	Chronic Fiscal Imbalances	Chronic Fiscal Imbalances	Extreme weather events	Extreme weather events
3rd	Chronic disease	Corruption	Rising greenhouse gas emission	Rising greenhouse gas emission	Unemployment & underemployment	Failure of National Governanace
4th	Fiscal crisis	Biodiversity loss	Cyber attacks	Water supply crisis	Climate change	State collapse or crisis
5th	Global Governance gaps	Climate Change	Water supply crisis	Management of population ageing	Cyber attacks	High structural unemployment or underemployment

Top 5 Global Risks In Terms Of Impact

	2010	2011	2012	2013	2014	2015
1st	Asset price collapse	Fiscal crisis	Major systematic financial failure	Major systematic financial failure	Fiscal crisis	Water crisis
2nd	Retrenchment from globalization (development)	Climate change	Water supply crisis	Water supply crisis	Climate change	Rapid and massive spread of infectious diseases
3rd	Oil Price spikes	Geopolitical conflict	Food shortage crisis	Chronic fiscal imbalances	Water crisis	Weapons of mass destruction
4th	Chronic Disease	Asset price collapse	Chronic fiscal imbalances	Diffusion of weapons of mass destruction	Unemployment and underemployment	Interstate conflict with regional consequences
5th	Fiscal Crisis	Extreme energy price volatility	Extreme volatility in energy & agricultural prices	Failure of climate change adaptation	Critical information infrastructure breakdown	Failure of climate change adaptation

In both charts, 2011 was a turning point with climate and environmental issues recognized as key risk factors to the economy. From 2011 onward, climate and environmental factors make up 44% of the direct risk factors in terms of Likelihood and 40% of the direct risk factors in terms of Impact on the global economy. In further examination of the charts, one can see where climate and environmental issues become key components and/or triggers of other economics risks such as volatility in agricultural prices, spread of disease, state collapse and crisis, and fiscal and employment issues. The cost of recovery from floods, droughts, and extreme weather events can be devastating to local economies and destabilizing to regional and/or national balance sheets. Changes in climate and environmental conditions that support the shift and expansion of the range for diseases can also disrupt economies as economic resources are shifted to meet the needs of changing priorities of public policy.

The U.S. military has parallel concerns to the World Economic Forum. The 2014 QDR identifies Climate Change as a threat multiplier.

> *Climate change poses another significant challenge for the United States and the world at large. As greenhouse gas emissions increase, sea levels are rising, average global temperatures are increasing, and severe weather patterns are accelerating. ...Climate change may exacerbate water scarcity and lead to sharp increases in food costs. The pressures caused by climate change will influence resource competition while placing additional burdens on economies, societies, and governance institutions around the world. These effects are threat multipliers that will aggravate stressors abroad such as poverty, environmental degradation, political instability, and social tensions–conditions that can enable terrorist activity and other forms of violence.*

—The 2014 Quadrennial Defense Review

SmarterSafer.org is a coalition of insurance companies, environmental organizations, and other allied members that recognize the need for a change in mindset and policy regarding natural disasters and extreme weather events.

> *Disasters are beginning to affect communities at an alarming pace, the result of increased development in harm's way as well as changing climate conditions.... Our current natural disaster policy framework focuses heavily on responding to disasters, rather than putting protective measures in place to reduce our vulnerability and limit a disaster's impact.*
>
> —SmarterSafer

We stand at the brink of unprecedented planetary ecological change, at least for the time modern humanity has lived on Earth. This is why the Earth Century is the largest context in which humanity must live and face the future.

We must create a visionary operating manual for This Spaceship Earth. That is the purpose of this book, to prompt the collective creation of that manual. The second, much more difficult step, is to then operate within the guidelines of this manual and to do so in the most expeditious way possible.

As discussed, we have operated beyond planetary equilibrium for 40 years. This means that even if everything changed now, if all carbon emissions stopped now in 2015, if all energy, water, and transportation usage were transformed now, we will still have significant ecological catastrophes ahead, for the next 70 years at a minimum. It has been locked in by what we have already, though largely unknowingly, wrought. That is why the period from 2015 to 2030 is a critical time. If, in this 15-year period, the majority of humanity can move to crew consciousness, we will be able to minimize the damage–economic, social, and ecological–done for the remainder of the century.

How we change and the amount of change, first in consciousness and thinking, and then into action in the next 15 years, will be the foundation for what TSE will look like as this century unfolds. This is perhaps one of the most high-level proactive versus reactive times in human history.

The first World Climate Conference took place in 1979. The focus of the discussion on the response to Climate Change was reducing CO_2 emissions. And so, 36 years later at COP21 (Conference of Parties) being held in Paris in late November through mid- December 2015, the discussion will again be the global response to Climate Change by reducing CO_2 emissions. COP21 is an international conference organized through the United Nations to establish international agreements on limiting greenhouse gas emissions to fulfill the IPCC (International Panel on Climate Change) agreements.

The following charts are based on a 2015 proposal for COP21 to reduce CO_2 emissions by 60% from the 2010 emission rate by 2050, starting in 2020. What does that mean?

The premise is that we need to reduce emissions. So what starting level should we use? In this case, the starting level is the 2010 emission level. The goal is to have the total global emissions be half of what they were in 2010 by 2050. It takes times to gear up policies and technologies to determine how each country wants to meet their reduced emission goals. Are you going to do it by reducing emissions, or by planting forests to absorb CO_2, or are you going to capture CO_2 in some other fashion? And, because of the time lag in developing the policies and methodologies, the clock on reduction will not start until 2020.

If we look at the Paris Proposal, the graph of reduction in CO_2 emissions looks like:

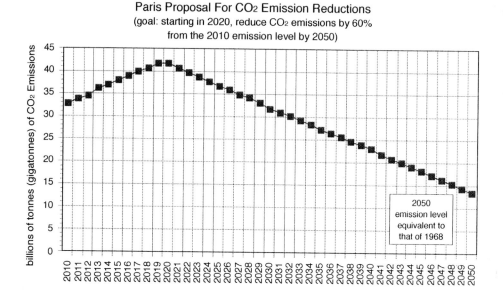

Paris Proposal For CO_2 Emission Reductions
(goal: starting in 2020, reduce CO_2 emissions by 60% from the 2010 emission level by 2050)

Looking at the chart, reducing emissions looks good. And, it certainly makes for understandable sound bites on the news, as well as giving citizens the hope that the issue of global warming and Climate Change are being taken seriously, and are potentially under control.

What the chart on emission reduction leaves out is what happens to the CO_2 that is released. As the next chart shows, cutting emissions simply slows the rate of increase for the amount of CO_2 entering the atmosphere.

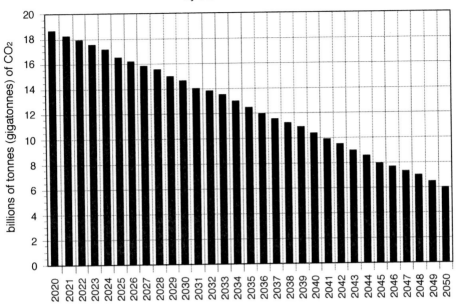

Annual Amount Of CO_2 Added To Atmosphere Per Year
by the Paris Plan

If CO_2 only stayed in the atmosphere for a year, the graph above would represent a trend we could find somewhat satisfactory. But, CO_2 stays in the atmosphere for decades to millennia. That means, we need to add all of the emitted CO_2 that will stay in the atmosphere together to really see the actual impact of the Paris Plan. And that graph looks like:

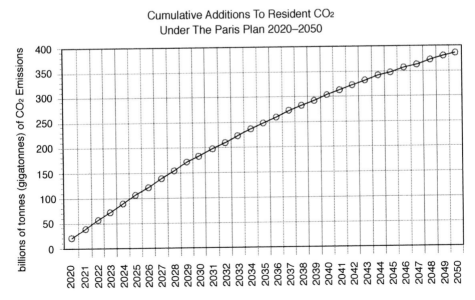

Cumulative Additions To Resident CO_2
Under The Paris Plan 2020–2050

The implication is that reducing emissions does not yield the result we are after and must have, if we want to lessen the severity of Climate Change and all of its attendant attributes of sea level rise, extreme weather events, crop failure, heat waves, forest fires, droughts, loss of glaciers and snow pack, as well as ocean acidification.

In fact, just stopping CO_2 emissions does not generate the results we need, because of the long time that CO_2 can stay–reside–in the atmosphere. Whatever the amount of CO_2 is in the atmosphere when we stop emitting anthropogenic CO_2 is the amount that will stay in the atmosphere for generations, as can be seen in this last graph.

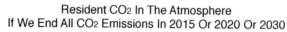

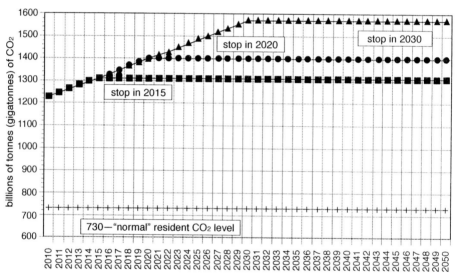

It will take a different mindset and approach to greenhouse gas emissions to solve the issue in a manner that is functional, fair, and beneficial to humanity's interdependence with TSE.

Chapter 7

RESIDENT CO_2: WE ARE A 730 SPECIES, LIVING IN A 1230 WORLD

When less is more

The current approach to resolving Climate Change is to focus on the reduction of CO_2 emissions. It is an understandable, yet insufficient approach. There is a lesson from childhood that applies to this topic, but it is a tough lesson to learn. The lesson is, ***being less bad is not the same as being good***.

2 °C

The general goal in international policy discussions regarding Climate Change agreements has been to reduce emissions of CO_2 so that the average global temperature increase does not surpass 2 °C (3.6 °F). The 2 °C idea was first put forth in 1970 by economist and Yale professor William Nordhaus. The rationale for the number was temperature increases above 2 °C would exceed the parameters of recorded and measured observations of climate for the past several hundred thousand years.

While 2 °C is a clear, concise, as well as measurable target, there is actually no guarantee that it is a safe goal. In 1990, The Stockholm Environment Institute did an analysis, and agreed that to avoid the worst impacts of Climate Change the limit should be 2 °C. But, of equal, if not greater importance, they also stated that:

> *Temperature increases beyond 1.0 °C may elicit rapid, unpredictable, and nonlinear responses that could lead to extensive ecosystem damage.*
>
> —S.E.I.

Focus on causes not symptoms

> *We often preoccupy ourselves with*
> *symptoms, whereas if we went to the root*
> *cause of the problem we would be able to*
> *overcome the problems once and for all.*
>
> —Wangari Maathai

In the climate conversation, we are suffering from misdirection. When CO_2 is released from any of multiple sources, it has one of three possible destinations. It will make its way into the ocean where it can be taken up by marine life or chemically react with seawater (27%). It can be absorbed into the biosphere via plants and microorganisms (28%). Or, it can take up residence in the atmosphere (45%).

> *I'm always struck by how successful we*
> *have been at hitting the bull's-eye of the*
> *wrong target.*
>
> —Joel Salatin

CO_2 emissions are the symptom—Resident CO_2 is the cause. Emissions are about what we toss up into the air. Whereas, it is the increase in Resident CO_2 that thickens the insulating and heat-trapping blanket that generates all the subsequent reactions of rising temperatures, rising seas, melting glaciers, and extreme weather events. This, then, causes displacement of people, loss of species, increased risk to public health, and jeopardizes economic stability, and social cohesion.

The wrong premise

The heart of the issue is not the emission of CO_2, but where CO_2 goes, and what it does when it gets there. Utilizing only CO_2 emission reductions as the acceptable mechanism to prevent future harm is an illusionary and false trail to a better future.

The same holds true for two other technical and economic approaches used in Climate Change discussions. The first is CAP and TRADE, and the second is Carbon Intensity.

In CAP and TRADE, a CAP is set on the amount of CO_2 (or other regulated emission) that can be emitted. Power plants are an example.

Depending upon the regulatory structure, the CAP can be allocated, or emissions credits can be purchased up to the level of the CAP. In any event, there is a CAP, a maximum amount of permitted emissions. In the instance of more efficient power plants, there is a reasonable probability that the emissions from the efficient plants are less than the CAP. Similarly, there is a reasonable probability that older and/or less efficient plants could have emissions that exceed the CAP. This is where TRADE comes into play. The more efficient power plant can sell its credits (emissions CAP – efficient plant emissions = credits) to the less efficient plant, so that the less efficient plant is now in compliance with the regulations (Emissions CAP > emissions + credits = regulatory compliance).

In CAP and TRADE, the operating premise is that the CAP will continually be lowered to cause all regulated entities to become more efficient and reduce their emissions. This would appear to be a very viable, market driven way to reduce greenhouse gas emissions, and thus deal with Climate Change, except for two events. First, CAP and TRADE is emissions focused, and has the potential in its early years to focus much more on trading emissions than reducing them. This, thereby, provides the possibility to reduce emissions on paper but not in reality. And second, the real need in mitigating the harm of Climate Change is dependent upon reducing the level of Resident CO_2 back to pre-industrial levels—and CAP and TRADE is not designed to confront that issue.

As to Carbon Intensity, it is the measure of CO_2 emissions of a country relative to its GDP (Gross Domestic Product—a measure of the nation's economic activity). *Functionally*, it is a measure of how efficiently a country is using fossil fuels to generate economic activity. If it took a theoretical country 8 tonnes of CO_2 emissions to generate $20,000 of revenue in the 1980s, but now that same country only needs 2 tonnes of CO_2 emissions to generate an equivalent amount of revenue, then its Carbon Intensity (CI) would be going down. If it took that same country 10 tonnes of CO_2 emissions to produce an equivalent amount of revenue, as it did in the 1980s with 8 tonnes of CO_2 emissions, its CI would be going up. There is a tendency for countries to refer to their CI when it is going down. That gives the impression that the increase in efficiency corresponds to a decrease in CO_2 emissions.

While there is no question that from the national level down to the individual, there is a great need for improving the efficiency and effectiveness of energy use—Carbon Intensity is a poor indicator of CO_2 emissions. Many energy sources can be used to generate revenue, and therefore, influence and increase a country's GDP. If the new revenue streams were powered by solar, wind, hydro, or nuclear energy sources, and absolutely no changes were made in fossil fuel use, the CI would go down because the GDP went up, while the CO_2 emissions stayed the same. A country could also update equipment and improve the efficiency of production while significantly growing its GDP. The CI would go down (generating less CO_2 emissions per unit of production), but have CO_2 emissions go up because of the overall increase in production (more plants, more manufacturing, etc.). As a result, Carbon Intensity is not a reliable unit of measure for CO_2 emissions. Remember, Carbon Intensity is emissions-focused, and does not deal with the real issue of Resident CO_2.

> *No matter what countries pledge in Paris,*
> *we'll still be on track for a 3-degree rise in*
> *global temperatures.*

—Christiana Figueres
    U.N. Climate Chief

> *For the Marshalls, for 39 atolls in the*
> *Federated States of Micronesia, for three*
> *atolls in Palau, for Maldives, for Tokelau–*
> *anything over 2 degrees is catastrophic.*

—Tony de Brum
    Foreign Minister of the Marshall Islands

Changing the metric

We now must change the language and the metrics of the discussion. We need to move from parts per million (ppm) of CO_2 and temperature rise, to billions of tonnes of CO_2.

In the remainder of the discussion, the new metric regarding CO_2 is weight, as in billions of tonnes. The reason for dialogue using tonnage instead of ppm (parts per million) is two-fold. The first explanation is that functionality, the data regarding anthropogenic CO_2 is given in tonnes (actually billions of tonnes or gigatonnes). Staying with tonnes makes for an easier, and smoother translation of the data to the graphics.

The second reason is that tonnage does a better job of demonstrating the scale of the issue, and helps clarify the relative values and timelines of different strategies of rectifying the situation.

Saying that the average annual increase of CO_2 in ppm this decade is 2.1ppm per year creates one perspective of the issue. And, saying that last year, CO_2 emissions were 36,000,000,000 tonnes creates another. Translating the tonnes of CO_2 emissions into an equivalent number of 4-ton elephants allows us to put an image in your mind of 273 elephants being launched into the air every second of everyday for the entire year. If one saw 273 elephants being shot into the atmosphere every second, surely that would generate a level of public awareness and discussion that is still lacking in the conversations regarding the seriousness of anthropogenic CO_2.

Since CO_2 is invisible, we cannot fully perceive the problem. We are now experiencing the disruptive attributes of the increase in Resident CO_2, but cannot see beyond the smoke stacks and tail pipes to grasp the heart of the issues. And, therein, lies the rub.

> *The ultimate measure of a man is not*
> *where he stands in moments of comfort*
> *and convenience, but where he stands at*
> *time of challenge and controversy.*
> —Martin Luther King Jr.

To fully comprehend the liability of only focusing on reducing emissions, we need to look at current levels of Resident CO_2 combined with the projected increase in Resident CO_2 resulting from the Paris Plan, if adopted.

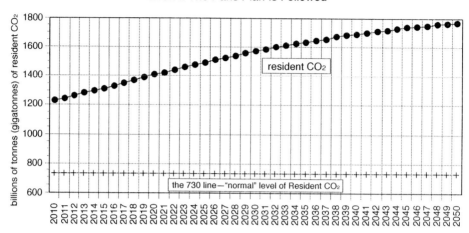

Cumulative Rise In Resident CO2 In The Atmosphere
Even If The Paris Plan Is Followed

resident CO2

the 730 line—"normal" level of Resident CO2

We are a 730 species living in a 1230 world

We are a 730 species who has created a 1230 world. What does that mean? The 730 refer to the 730 gigatonnes (billion of tons) of CO_2 that has been resident in the atmosphere during the development of our species, our civilizations, and our understanding of the world. It is the amount of CO_2 in the atmosphere that gave us the weather, seasons, and climate that we think of as normal. The 1230 refer to the current tonnage of Resident CO_2 in the atmosphere in 2015 that we humans have caused to be there by our cumulative, collective, and continuous activities since the onset of the industrial revolution.

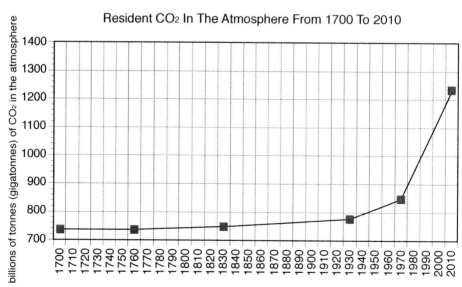

Resident CO2 In The Atmosphere From 1700 To 2010

Keep in mind that modern humans, homo sapiens, have inhabited the earth for 200,000 years. Yet, it has taken less than a 100 years for us to generate an atmosphere not witnessed on this planet for at least 800,000 years. We are now living in a planetary environment outside the historical and biological context of our species and our cultural heritage.

It is also worth noting that the dramatic increase in Resident CO_2 has occurred simultaneous with the first photo of the whole earth, Earth Day, and the beginning of the environmental movement. It is also congruent with the continuing increase in temperature, and the now familiar symptoms of Climate Change we experience today.

Is this really the trend we want to promote, and continue? Is it truly in our best interest to stay on our current path?

> *Soon, everyone will have to make the choice between what is right and what is easy.*
>
> —Professor Dumbledore

Resolution

To resolve all the issues connected to Climate Change and global warming the focus needs to be on reducing the resident level of CO_2 in the atmosphere.

> *We can't solve problems by using the same kind of thinking we used when we created them.*
>
> —Albert Einstein

Reducing Resident CO_2 requires a many faceted, integrated systems approach. The central mechanisms will incorporate:

1. enhancing and restoring the integrity of biological systems on TSE so that they can uptake more CO_2.
2. developing technologies that uptake CO_2 and/or convert CO_2 into other molecules and elements that reduce heat capture in the atmosphere.
3. reducing, and eventually eliminating CO_2 pollution from anthropogenic sources.

What would life be if we had no courage to attempt anything?

—Vincent van Gogh

We are a 730 species in need of a moonshot

It has taken us 45 years to spike the CO_2 level in the atmosphere—so the question before us, do we have the commitment, the willingness, the technological, scientific, educational, social, economic, environmental wherewithal to undo the harm in the same 45 year time frame? Can we reduce Resident CO_2 to 800 gigatonnes by 2060? Can we reach an equilibrium level of Resident CO_2 of 730–750 gigatonnes by 2065?

Yes, we can. And, it will be a moonshot.

In May of 1961, President Kennedy stood before Congress and said:

> *This nation should commit itself to achieving the goal, before the decade is out, of landing a man on the moon and returning him safely to the earth.*

At that time, the United States had less than 16 minutes of experience with an astronaut in suborbital space flight. Consider that for a moment. The country had yet to put an astronaut into orbit around our home planet, and the president was calling for landing a man on the moon in 8 years time. He was asking Congress for funding to create technologies that had yet to exist, train people to do what had never been done, and send people to places no one had ever been, safely and quickly. The word moonshot has been in our vocabulary ever since.

Moonshots are diametrically opposed to Hail Mary passes. Hail Mary passes are born of desperation and have little chance of success. Moonshots are ambitious, dedicated, and groundbreaking undertakings that yield success.

Do we know how to do that in 2015? No, we don't. No one did in 1961 either, yet the goal was achieved in July 1969 when Neil Armstrong stepped onto the lunar surface.

We will need to invent new technologies and materials to accomplish this goal. We will need to scale up current non-polluting technologies and methodologies in transportation, energy, agriculture, housing, manufacturing, and design. We will integrate natural systems and services into our infrastructure both directly and through bio/eco-mimicry. We will redefine and reshape the economy at an even faster rate than the current *disruptive* technologies. But, those so-called disruptive technologies and ideas are really harbingers of the future. We are a dynamic species on a dynamic planet.

We will create technologies to remove CO_2 from the atmosphere, to aggressively vacuum or retrieve the deadly waste we have put there in the last 100 years. Atmospheric Cleansing technology will be essential. This technology is in the early stages of development, as this book is being written. It must be scaled up in the 2020s. The economic incentives will be overwhelming. In the short term of 2015–2030, vast sums of money will come to those that successfully develop and then deploy such technologies. The value of such technologies goes way beyond that. The sooner this technology can be deployed, the less human suffering and economic damage there will be in the Earth Century. These will be technologies that will literally save tens of millions of lives, and prevent tens of trillions of dollars of economic loss. These incentives were not part of the first moonshot, so the probability of developing and implementing such technologies has more thrust behind it than what led Armstrong to set foot on the moon.

We will create these technologies because we have to, and because we want to. We are in a race against ourselves, at the moment. We can continue to increase our disequilibrium with TSE and promote devastating Climate Change, or we can reconceptualize, redefine, and redesign our relationship with TSE, and operate in a context that promotes the longevity of humanity and civilization on TSE.

The difference between the effort to land a man on the moon and reducing Resident CO_2 back to 800 gigatonnes is similar; things will need to be done that have never been done. The huge difference was that Kennedy's challenge, while it created a vision around which a country and a world could coalesce, was a major scientific effort that had many benefits. Reducing Resident CO_2 in the atmosphere to a level of 800 gigatonnes by mid-century is about the survival of life and civilization as we have come to know it.

We can complain about the choices we have given ourselves. But, we need to remember that we, collectively, cumulatively, and continuously have created the choices we have before us. We have focused on the symptom—the economy. In our actions, we have neglected the welfare of the source of our life and life-ways, TSE. Too often, we forget that TSE is the only island in the universe where we can live and sustain ourselves. We have confused exchangeable with interchangeable. Buying $5.00 worth of groceries provides a very different nutritional and culinary experience than eating a $5.00 bill. Similarly, our vehicles will take us much farther on $20.00 worth of fuel than simply putting a $20.00 bill in the tank.

infinite gratitude for the past infinite
service to the present infinite
responsibility to the future

—task of Zen Buddhists

We are going to be held accountable and responsible for our common fate. Are we going to continue to put ourselves at risk, or are we going to do right by future generations?

The rights of prosperity are more
important than the desires of the present.

—Fredrick Law Olmstead

What can this moonshot do?

It has been 45 years from 1970 to 2015. This is the time when Resident CO_2 went from 830 to 1230GT. Humanity has, therefore, increased Resident CO_2 by approximately 9GT a year. The task ahead is to reduce Resident CO_2 by that much per year for the next 45 years, so that we can get back to 800GT by 2060.

It is clear, that between 2015–2020, this will not happen. This means that starting in the 2020s, we must show reductions per year, and these annual reductions must increase every year to meet the goal by 2060. So again, we are put into the 2015–2030 time frame to completely turn around the root cause of Climate Change, if we want to have our grandchildren experience life and civilization as we know it today or an even better world than today.

It is also clear that during this CO_2 reduction moonshot, there will be continued Climate Change that will cause suffering, death, relocation, and multi-trillion dollar economic losses between 2015–2060. At this time, we cannot explain or predict how we can accelerate the moonshot efforts, but we can if the critical mass of TSE crew consciousness occurs rapidly.

Here is a chart showing what reduction of Resident CO_2 will look like for the moonshot goal of 800GT by 2060.

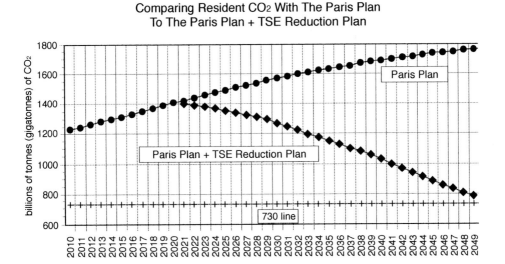

Many future generations will look back at this chart and realize that it turned out to be very pessimistic and conservative.

Now, we move on and look toward what we can collectively, and individually, do as we embrace TSE crew consciousness.

Chapter 8

THINGS HUMANITY CAN DO AND THE URGENT NEED TO DO THEM

In the Earth Century chapter, we saw how taking action soon can change the ongoing and accelerating damage that is facing humanity on TSE. In the last chapter, we presented the stark reality that humanity and tens of thousands of other species are at high risk, unless and until we reduce the amount of Resident CO_2 in the atmosphere. We suggest that humanity must act as crew as soon as possible, certainly a majority of us by 2025 to 2030. We saw that even if all greenhouse gas emissions stopped tomorrow, we would still have decades of warming, sea level rise, melting glaciers, and species extinction.

> *The Department of Defense sees climate change as a present security threat. Although climate-related stress will disproportionately affect fragile and conflict-affected states, even resilient, well-developed countries are subject to the effects of climate change in significant and consequential ways.*
>
> —National Security Implications of Climate-Related Risks and a Changing Climate, 23 July 2015

We are really looking at minimizing human suffering, catastrophic economic losses, and large-scale, geo-political disruption. While humanity is currently moving on a course that would bring all of these negatives to fruition, we have also been developing technologies and consciousness that could provide for a significantly more positive outcome. What we cannot do is travel both paths simultaneously.

> *We stand now where two roads diverge. But unlike the roads in Robert Frost's familiar poem, they are not equally fair. The road we have long been traveling is deceptively easy, a smooth super highway*

on which we progress with great speed,
but at its end lies disaster. The other fork
of the road—the one less traveled by—
offers our last, our only chance to reach a
destination that assures the preservation of
the earth.

—Rachel Carson

To avoid ever-larger suffering by the species living on TSE, humanity simply must change its ways before 2030. With crew consciousness, we can attempt transformative, large-scale initiatives to minimize as much as possible future catastrophes. We owe this to ourselves, our children, our grandchildren, our great grandchildren, and to all the species we are endangering. Whether our efforts are successful, or a delaying tactic of the catastrophic, is a function of how many of us operate from the perspective of crew consciousness, and do so in the near term.

Humanity has never faced the global climate realities we now face. This means that we have no precedent or road map to use going forward. We must do something that is hard for all of us, which is to fundamentally and radically change—and fast! That is the key to collectively, and cumulatively, implementing the large-scale changes that are needed relative to our current *modus operandi.*

Saving civilization is not a spectator sport.
We all have to get involved.

—Lester Brown

In the last chapter about Resident CO_2, we presented the true metric humanity must address if we all want to avoid unprecedented catastrophes. As TSE crew, we must all orient our visions, our plans, and most importantly our coordinated execution of them to find a way back to 800 gigatonnes of Resident CO_2 in the Earth's atmosphere. We can get there. The question is when?

If we do not try, civilization as we know it, and our way of life will no longer be an option by the end of this Earth Century. Even if we get back to 800 gigatonnes of Resident CO_2 by 2050, there will be massive social, economic, and political disruption. The question facing us is… do we want to minimize that by accelerating the rate of Resident CO_2 reduction. This is the choice we have, yes or no.

Changing consciousness comes first. When consciousness is changed, thinking changes, the ways of seeing reality changes, and the legacy priorities and previous ways of thinking disintegrate.

> *It isn't enough to do our best, sometimes*
> *we have to do what is required.*

—Winston Churchill

We must see the current reality of TSE without the blinders of politics, religion, source of employment, vested interests, nationality, or assumed convenience. Humanity has never done this. That will give comfort to those who want to be able to say that we can't change.

In reality, the history of humanity is about doing things that went against traditional thinking or were thought impossible. We have been able to:

- set sail across the great oceans and didn't fall off the edge of the flat Earth as expected.
- run a sub-four minute mile, once thought impossible, and now commonplace.
- accomplish manned flight.
- land on the moon.
- split the atom.
- double our life expectancy in two centuries.

WE CAN do what has never been done.

> *We choose to go to the moon in this decade*
> *and do the other things, not because*
> *they are easy, but because they are hard,*
> *because that goal will serve to organize*
> *and measure the best of our energies*
> *and skills, because that challenge is one*
> *that we are willing to accept, one we are*
> *unwilling to postpone, and one which we*
> *intend to win.*

—John Fitzgerald Kennedy

In this case, the goal is even greater, for it is a matter of survival. Human civilization and survival may well be the context for moving forward as it trumps politics, religion, economics, policy, and nationalism.

We have to understand that we must look at everything from a systems approach (one of R. Buckminster Fuller's strongest points) with survival and the long-term viability of civilization, as we know it, at stake. The re-education and re-training of the work force is an example. If we want to stop the use of fossil fuels, we must first decide how to best retrain and transition workers in this industry. There are tens-of-thousands of people that work in the fossil fuels industries. They need to be retrained for the new renewable and alternative energy industries. There are coal, petroleum, and natural gas states in the U.S. where opposition to fundamental change is resisted because of the levels of unemployment and negative economic consequences.

To change such opposition, there must be a crew consciousness of proactive transitioning of fossil fuel workers in these states. In provinces, states, and countries globally, there need to be underlying compassionate acceptance that we are all in this together. We must be smart about helping everyone through this unprecedented and disruptive transition. There is a dramatic need for workers to rebuild and create infrastructure, new energy platforms, and new technological undertakings on a grand scale. As old industries and ways of doing things recede into history, we all have to help those in these industries move to the new ways necessary at this time of crisis.

> *The illiterate of the 21st century will not be those who cannot read and write, but those who cannot learn, unlearn, and relearn.*
> —Alvin Toffler

There will be places and nations in the world that can dramatically decrease the use of fossil fuels sooner than others. This must be coordinated so that the net result is a reduction in usage and emissions, globally. European countries, Canada, and the United States will be able to convert from fossil fuels to alternative and renewable energies faster than poorer developing countries. Accordingly, the TSE metric prescribes that this must all be calculated so that the only measurement is usage, decline, and ultimately non-use of practices that put greenhouse gases into our preciously thin atmosphere.

As crew members of TSE, we can do what is discussed in this and the next chapter. As status quo passengers, we cannot. If your crew

84

consciousness is developing, then you will see that what we suggest here, can be done and must be done.

What follows is not a comprehensive list. There will be many other undertakings that others will think of and/or create. We invite that discussion at www.thisspaceshipearth.org, which we hope will become a global clearinghouse for growing TSE crew consciousness. We want to involve everyone, every entity, cause, non-profit, investors, company, and government to think and act ever more in TSE crew consciousness. Consider this as a starter list of imperatives that we can, at least, move on—with urgency.

Redefine "Sustainability" as operating TSE at 1.0 or < 1.0

From a TSE consciousness operating TSE at 1.0 or <1.0 planetary footprint, can be the only definition of sustainability. The goal would be to attain this level by 2030. Any other use of the word *sustainability* to describe a building or project is to perpetuate silo thinking, for no entity can be sustainable on its own. Sustainability, if it is to be achieved, is a systems measurement at a planetary level. Humanity is not living sustainably until we get back to and then under 1.0, globally. Simple math and logic point to this being the only global measurement. There is only one Planet Earth, and we are either living within its context, or we are not. If we are, then humanity has attained sustainability. However, we are currently operating at a TSE of 1.6.

The most public metric of our path to sustainability is the date of Earth Overshoot Day, the day of the year when we cross over the 1.0 threshold of planetary renewable resource consumption and pollution absorption. In 2015, Earth Overshoot Day was August 13th. We need to start moving that date back, and cannot rest until that date is December 31. Then, the next part of the journey, for centuries-long sustainability, begins.

Decrease fossil fuel usage ASAP

The use of fossil fuels is the single greatest cause of global warming and Climate Change. To slow warming, and then to eliminate on-going warming, it is imperative that human use of fossil fuels decline as much and as fast as possible. This is perhaps the single most important area for humanity to act with complete urgency. This will be very difficult

85

as global society, and the global economy are largely based upon the use of fossil fuels. Fortunately, we now have a confluence of trends and dynamics that give us a path to a dramatic decrease in usage and resultant greenhouse warming. Keep in mind that global society and the global economy are really in need of energy, not fossil fuel, *per se*.

As a futurist, the author, David Houle has been consistently accurate in his forecasts about energy, the price of oil and new energy models. He recently forecast that 2015 may well be the peak year of fossil fuel usage due to a confluence of trends. We, therefore, start with the unprecedented reality that the year this book is being published is the threshold between ever increasing use of fossil fuels—and therefore emissions of the same- and the beginning of the decline of usage. This is a good place to start.

Some of the significant efforts to lower use of fossil fuel would be:

- Fossil fuel companies no longer think of themselves as fossil fuel companies, but think of themselves as energy companies. They owe this to all their stakeholders. The well-known example here is that the railroad companies missed the future, because they thought they were in the train business, not the transportation business. Had they thought otherwise, they might have funded the Wright Brothers and been the first airline companies, or even the first major automotive companies.

- Fossil fuel companies move to all forms of alternative and renewable energy. This will be facilitated by the reality of the low price of oil, globally. As of 2015, it is highly likely we may never see $100 barrel oil again. Given that most of the easy oil has been extracted. The further out and deeper we go into the ocean, the higher the cost of extraction. Consequently, the oil companies have great economic incentive to move into the inevitable and explosively growing alternative and renewable energy business.

- If in fact, it becomes clear that 2015 is the peak year for fossil fuel use, the financial community will face the fossil fuel industries and ask them directly if they are going to change their energy production profile to align with the 21st century, not the 20th. If they will not change, the financial community will either put them into the category of short-term investment or ask them to dramatically increase dividends to maintain share price. Simply put, there is more wealth creation opportunity in alternative and renewable energy than any other business in history. It is the first time that 6+ billion people use something that has to be replaced. Wealth creation can, therefore, be a key driver to move away from fossil fuels.

- Taxing fossil fuel usage, a simple carbon tax not an exchange, would act to make us all aware of the cost of carbon. This would be an economic disincentive to use fossil fuels at every stage of the process, from the ground to finished product process. This is not just for the consumption of oil and gas, but also for the use of petroleum in the production of plastics and any other commodity where fossil fuels are used in the generation of the product.

- The historic model, technology, and mind trap of energy distribution has been based on large centralized power production facilities with long transmission lines to deliver the electricity to the user. However, new technologies allow the focus of energy systems to be based on on-site capture and storage for current and future use.

- Accelerate distributed energy grids using renewable energy with its own battery storage. This will lower demand, spread demand more evenly, minimize massive damage due to cyber attack, lessen business losses due to loss of electricity from extreme weather, and make both AC and DC integral parts of electricity. Wind and solar will be used to power the production of the batteries, which then store wind and solar for the charging of electric automobiles, and household energy use. This must be done at both the personal and corporate level. As this book is being written, Elon Musk built on the transformative legacy of Tesla Motors to introduce Tesla Energy's Power Pack and Power Wall. This is the first time that a major company has utilized alternative and renewable energy from beginning to end product. Tesla Energy has received over one billion dollars of potential business from registered, interested purchasers in the first two months since announcement, mostly coming from larger entities. The marketplace is ready.

Tesla and any other companies that come into this space will need support to build the scale essential for significant fossil fuel reduction. There will be ever more evolved, including efficient battery technologies that will be able to capture sun and solar power. All these technologies, and the companies that create them, will need significant investment and perhaps initial government support so that scale can rapidly be reached.

- TSE crew should continue to install solar panels with new leasing and rental financing to accelerate installations. The same is true for large and small-scale wind turbines.

- Building codes need to be updated to allow retrofitting of existing buildings, which would constantly increase efficiency. These conservation and efficiency efforts must be combined with moving to stored renewable energy to power homes, offices, and factories.
- Create new forms of housing and buildings that are energy neutral, or energy positive. Crew consciousness is now the starting point of design.
- Crew needs to put forth general efforts to conserve energy through efficiency.
- Retrofitting of personal transport should move away from fossil fuels, so at least 60% of vehicles on TSE do not use fossil fuels by 2030.
- Public transport should be retrofitted so that 100% of the crew do not use fossil fuels by 2030.
- Plastic should be taxed, since it is largely petroleum based. The crew should find or develop other constructive fully biodegradable or reusable components to be utilized.

Completely rethink agriculture and implement those changes as fast as possible

Move to vertical gardens, local gardens, and plant land to generate complete meals rather than mono-crops.

The 20th century industrialized agriculture model, so prevalent today, must be dispensed with as quickly as possible; it is the epitome of silo thinking. Not only will it no longer serve the expansion and relocation of population growth, industrialized agriculture is in itself a major contributor to global warming with massive amounts of greenhouse gases released. It is also detrimental to our survival as it depletes the soil resources we have. Raising animals and farming create more greenhouse emissions than transportation.

Reintegrate livestock with regenerative farming. This will dramatically cut down on greenhouse gas emissions, and increase productivity and profit for livestock ranchers and farmers. This will also create meat without growth hormones, antibiotics, disease-causing bacteria, and can have increased nutritional value. There are many examples of farms and farmers who have successfully made the transition to a systems-based agricultural model, and have the financials to prove its viability.

As society moves toward 2045, when it is expected that 70% of 9 billion people will be living in urban environments, moving agriculture closer to where people are will be critical. We can no longer afford to spend significant amounts of energy to move food long distances, nor can we accept the spoilage of food resulting from its transportation time. A primary solution is to have a huge scale-up of vertical gardens. These vertical gardens can be in urban areas. This means less transport, which means both greater freshness, and less carbon emissions. In addition, indoor vertical gardens can have 2–3 crop cycles per year, and can be largely grown hydroponically. Therefore, worldwide topsoil is not diminished. Indoor vertical gardens will not need pesticides, herbicides, or any such damaging chemical. Why would we not want to move to this form of farming, ASAP? We can take currently existing buildings of low economic value, such as empty factories and closed big box stores, and create thousands of indoor vertical gardens that can also be energy and carbon neutral.

Launch a global initiative to retrofit and redesign buildings in all forms

In 2013, 48% of all energy use in the United States was by buildings, which created the greatest category of fossil fuel usage. The number is even higher globally. The vast majority of existing buildings have not been constructed with energy efficiency or low carbon footprint in mind. Certainly, they were not built with crew consciousness. Various estimates put rapid energy reduction savings of 25% for a full scale, coordinated effort to conserve, retrofit, and utilize environmentally friendly ideas into the building stock. Going forward, there needs to be a high benchmark for energy efficient buildings, carbon neutral buildings, and smaller ecofriendly personal dwellings. These efforts are already well underway, but need to be quickly expedited.

Support Tesla Energy, Tesla Motors, Solar City, and any companies that have a proven business vision to eliminate the use of fossil fuels

Economic policy must support any industry that, scaled up, can eliminate fossil fuel use, and greenhouse gas emissions. The hope is that hundreds of companies similar to Tesla will launch and grow between 2015 and 2020 with popular and governmental support so that all can be scaled up in the 2020s.

These companies will be in transportation, energy, construction, farming, manufacturing, and any industry that has a large reliance on fossil fuels.

It is well past time to move the massive amount of subsidies paid to the fossil fuel industry to these new emerging renewable energy companies. From 2002-2008 in the United States, there was $72.5 billion dollars of federal government subsidies paid to the fossil fuel industry. During this same time, $12.2 billion was paid to renewables. In other words, the fossil fuel industry received 6 times, or 600% more subsidies than renewable energy did over this six-year period. Why should energy companies from the past 2 centuries get more subsidies than the energy companies and entities shaping 21st energy?

Move to a TSE crew consciousness on population growth

Once we think of ourselves as crew of TSE, then we start to think of every birth as an additional crewmember that has to be supported. They need food, water, shelter, education, employment, and have an inherent right to a life of dignity.

> *Human beings are good at many things,*
> *but thinking of our species as a whole is*
> *not one of our strong points.*
> —David Attenborough

We need to consider population, not just at the individual or family level, but also at TSE level. Is reaching a population of 9 billion a goal we want to achieve or an outcome of not seeing ourselves in a one-planet context? What is the balance point we want to strike between birth rate, longevity, resource capability, and TSE capacity? While there is no simple, immediate, acceptable, universal answer to the issue that does not mean that the topic can be or should be ignored. Humanity is the driver of the changes we are seeing on TSE. Answers to questions are going to be directly related to the number of people on TSE. So sooner (preferably) or later, we have to face forward to the question of our own number.

Remember, there is as much fresh water in the world today as there was a million years ago. Yet, there are more than 7.3 billion people alive at the writing of this book using that same amount of water and land that existed when there were just one million of us. So, population and population growth is one of the key issues facing TSE. We must collectively and systemically find moral and ethical ways to inhabit TSE. Survival trumps beliefs, and we need to place population growth and over population, clearly into the discussion of how we achieve a sustainability level of TSE < 1.

Develop a global systems approach to energy, agriculture, and emissions

We have common, yet differentiated responsibilities, which is to say that different countries are starting from different places in 2015. However, it is only through a global—not nationalistic—viewpoint that can we collaborate as crew to solve these problems. Every country must move as quickly as it can to reverse and resolve. But, not every country has the same capability or capacity to adapt alternative methodologies, nor are all countries equally culpable for the harm that has been done to the life support system of TSE.

> *Trust, but verify.*
> —Ronald Reagan

There will need to be openness and transparency in the process of achieving TSE < 1. This may mean creating a new global monitoring entity whose sole mission is to monitor, measure, and disseminate to humanity the continually updated Global System plan. That information would then be used to plan, coordinate, and implement strategies to improve the rate at which all countries fulfill their planetary responsibilities to reach TSE < 1.

Redefine work

This would entail rapidly moving away from the everyone-in-one-place-at-the-same-time Industrial Age model that largely governs work in the current global economy. The transportation and energy consequences of the format are highly detrimental to TSE, public health, and individual welfare. Yes, much of work is social and interactive. We should focus on the fact that we want to promote the social and interactive, but do not want rush hour (a misnomer if there ever was one) and traffic congestion based on a one-person, one-vehicle transportation model. A systems approach could be readily applied to redefining and re-conceptualizing work. We can use multi-modal transportation systems—from ride sharing, Lyft and Uber, greenways and bikes, to a wide range of public and private transportation combined with new or rediscovered urban redesigns to move people. There is also the use of digital communication in which technology can minimize the need for actually moving people, when what needs to be moved… are ideas.

Make this a new bottom-line metric. Develop metrics of working around the declining use of anything that creates greenhouse emissions, or uses non-recycled or non-recyclable resources.

Plan for strategic retreat

Accept that sea level rise will force many people to have to relocate, and plan for this in advance. Then, this is strategic and not reactive.

Even if all greenhouse gas emissions were to cease at the end of 2015, we already have so much Resident CO_2 in our preciously thin atmosphere that we will have displacement of millions of people and the loss of hundreds of billions of dollars in land and real estate value along ocean coastlines alone. Factor in the increasing disruption of extreme weather and those numbers go up. This is already baked into the atmosphere due to the increase from 730 to 1230 gigatonnes of CO_2 in the last two centuries.

Since it is clear that greenhouse gas emissions will continue for at least another 15 years at the optimum, and that this will increase Resident CO_2 in the atmosphere as shown earlier, the numbers will be staggering. Strategic retreat is the anticipatory planning for the tens of millions of displaced people around the world and the staggering economic losses that will occur. Even if we fully stop emissions by 2030, and that is not very likely without TSE crew consciousness, the current projections of sea level rise, present catastrophic and destabilizing numbers by 2050:

- Tens of millions of Bangladeshi citizens will have to move, as their land will be underwater.
- Millions of Americans will have to retreat from south Florida and most of the coastal areas of the Atlantic and Gulf coasts.
- Tens of trillions of dollars will be lost through the disappearance of land, real estate, and commerce in the U.S. alone.

- There will an overwhelming cost associated with the rebuilding of major shipping ports, whose infrastructure will no longer exist or work.
- Where will we relocate the island nations of the world, such as the Seychelles and French Polynesia, whose homelands will vanish?

These are real issues and situations that are going to happen, not events that will happen if we do not change.

Here is a look at the top 20 cities vulnerable to sea level rise.

Climate Change Warning: 20 Cities With The Most To Lose From Rising Seas

Risk Priority	City	Population at risk (in millions)
1	Guangzhou, China	14.2
2	Mumbai, India	23.7
3	Kolkata, India	16.7
4	Guayaquil, Ecuador	2.7
5	Shenzhen, China	14.2
6	Miami, FL. USA	6.8
7	Tianjin, China	10.9
8	New York City & Newark, New Jersey	23
9	Ho Chi Minh City, Vietnam	8.5
10	New Orleans, LA, USA	1.5
11	Jakarta, Indonesia	11.6
12	Abidjan, Ivory Coast	5.9
13	Chennai, India	11.3
14	Surat, India	4.6
15	Zhanjiang, China	7.0
16	Tampa-St. Petersburg, Fla. USA	2.8
17	Boston, MA, USA	5.5
18	Bangkok, Thailand	10.3
19	Xiamen, China	3.6
20	Nagoya, Japan	9.1
	Total at risk	193.9

Given the Resident CO_2 of 1230 gigatonnes that is already in the atmosphere, and the certainty that this number will increase at least for a decade, all of these cities will suffer some amount of economic losses and population relocation. To the degree humanity does not take actions towards ending emissions as well as simultaneously extracting CO_2 from the atmosphere by 2030, ensures that the economic losses, social upheaval, and population relocations in just these cities alone will be unprecedented and catastrophic.

As this book is about to go to press, one of the top stories in the world is the massive numbers of refugees leaving the Middle East and Africa for Europe and other parts of the world. The numbers are staggering, and the greatest since WWII. There has been no planning or preparation for this wave of refugees and immigrants. The actual sense of national and continental identity in Europe is being questioned. The way to put the need for advance planning for Strategic Retreat in perspective is that by 2025 there will be 10 to 20 times the number of sea level rise refugees each year as have been created in 2015. Think, 10-20 million people a year needing relocation annually on TSE.

In any country that has sea level rise issues, there simply must be a private and public sector collaboration to plan for these unprecedented realities. The consequences of what could happen if this eventuality is not organized are almost incomprehensible to consider. Massive migration, total loss of land and real estate, a collapse of national GDP, and a social unrest leading to political unrest are reasonable to consider as possibilities. So strategic planning for such probable realities needs to begin.

It is these possibilities that are the counter argument to any individual, company, or government who states that the costs of weaning ourselves from fossil fuel usage, and changing the way we do things has too much of an economic cost. Those costs will be completely inconsequential when compared to the cost of hundreds of millions of displaced persons, and the loss of tens of trillions of dollars globally. A reality check, humanity has never faced a calamity of this size. We must start to plan for this, as we simultaneously work to minimize it through TSE crew consciousness.

Beginning national and global plans for strategic retreat is essential. Coining the Boy Scout motto: Be Prepared!

Water

We have to completely change the way we use and look at water. Water is potentially the most mentally invisible resource that we use, and are in contact with everyday. We mentally disconnect the water that is used to grow our food from:

- the water that generates the electricity for our homes and offices,
- the water that comes out of the tap,
- the water used to make every object that we use,
- the water we used yesterday,
- the water we want tomorrow,
- the water in the lakes, ponds, rivers and streams,
- the water at the beach, in the rain, the ocean, the ice and snow, and
- the water we just flushed away.

There is only one water. Earth, currently, has the same amount of fresh water with 7.3 billion people as it did hundreds of thousands of years ago when there were only a few million. We have to look at water for what it is, essential for life. We can no longer think of it as waste or something to be used once. We can no longer use water for industrial production and industrial agriculture the way we do. We need to learn to use water more effectively and efficiently–at a personal level, as well as in business, industry, and agriculture. We need to stop supporting products and services that are created with a wasteful consciousness relative to water.

New zoning laws must be instituted for water. Rain is to be captured for local use not considered run-off in our overly paved landscape. Nature does not have storm run-offs or rain drains. We need to stop thinking of water as causing problems, but as something that is vital to our lives and our communities. We need to sequence water use and match water quality with its intended use. All too often, the dog is the only one that gets the joke that the water in your toilet and the water from the faucet currently come from the same water pipe—it's the same water. With some changes in plumbing regulations, homes and business can be plumbed so that potable water goes for potable uses, water contaminated with human waste goes to waste water treatment and not-potable, non-waste contaminated water can be used for irrigation or other appropriate purposes. Currently, domestic water use in the USA is approximately

100 gallons of potable water per day. That number is driven by how we plumb, not by the intended use of water. Most, if not all, urban communities in the USA, currently, fight fires with potable water.

As of the writing of this book, the costs of desalination of salt water are still high. It also has many negative consequences such as what to do with the waste. We must explore and create new ways to desalinate with no negative side effects, and at ever-lower costs. Since fresh water is now becoming a commodity that people fight over, and that causes social unrest, desalination must be invested in and scaled up, in sound environmental ways.

Unfortunately, our thinking of fresh water as unlimited has put us in the position that there will be severe droughts, lawsuits, and even limited wars over water in the coming years. We must change our consciousness about water. *Our survival depends on it.*

Remember the old adage that a human might be able to go weeks without food, days without water, and minutes without oxygen. We live on a planet where we have poisoned our food, depleted our fresh water, and polluted the air we breathe. We are damaging the three things we all need to live, to survive.

The seas

The theory of evolution and general science says that all life on Earth has come from the oceans. The seas are the source of life on Earth. Yet, we have completely disregarded this thinking in our relationship to the oceans. We dump toxic chemicals, massive amounts of plastic in all shapes and sizes, and other pollutants into our oceans in an ongoing process. That must stop.

In addition, we have so over fished the oceans that we are approaching a critical junction. The total amount of animal life in the oceans has dropped by 70% since we passed the 1.0 resource footprint some 40 years ago. This must change. It is hard to see how we can go forward without at least a 2–4 year moratorium on large-scale industrial fishing and the expansion of marine reserves and sanctuaries. This will cause great economic havoc that we can anticipate, and for which we can plan. We need to find alternative incomes for fishermen. and the fishing industry. We need to dramatically increase the amount of safely farmed fish in the world.

We have destroyed vast amounts of our coral reefs through pollution, plastic and toxic waste, and ocean acidification. These magnificent ecosystems must be protected. A lesser model of the ocean strategy must also be put in place in all lakes and rivers around the world.

Humanity cannot live long with dead seas.

> *No blue, no green*
> —Sylvia Earle

Transportation

Transportation represents 13% of all greenhouse gas emissions globally in 2004, 34% in the United States, which has dropped to 28% by 2013. This is a good sign, but was largely due to the dramatic drop in miles driven during the 2008–2011 great recession. This is a very significant area for conscious change. Our personal vehicles are a major cause of global warming. Collectively, cars and trucks account for nearly one-fifth of *all* U.S. emissions, emitting around 24 pounds of carbon dioxide and other global-warming gases for every gallon of gas. About 5 pounds come from the extraction, production, and delivery of the fuel, while the great bulk of heat-trapping emissions—more than 19 pounds per gallon—comes right out of a car's tailpipe. Did you know that every gallon you burn puts that many emissions into the atmosphere? Now you do. Welcome to your developing crew consciousness.

The good news is that transportation is one of the areas where we see the beginnings of the necessary revolution to eliminate fossil fuel usage. This is one of the few areas where TSE crew members are already to make a difference.

Hybrid cars and plug-in electric cars are at the beginning of rapid growth. Hydrogen fuel-cell cars will be coming online in a number of countries. The use of rapid transit increased dramatically during the Great Recession, and the numbers have stayed at a historical high level. Rapid transit has a lower per capita level of greenhouse gas emissions than automobiles. In the U.S. alone, 10.8 billion trips were taken on public transportation in 2013, which is the highest number in 58 years.

We must remember what happened in the 20th century. The inventions that occurred during the century became institutionalized. The internal combustion engine quickly became the definition of transportation. Now, in the 21st century, we must reinvent transport with new forms of energy and create new means of transport. There are simply too many cars that exhaust greenhouse gases into the atmosphere.

Currently, there are a bit more than one billion automobiles being driven in the world. About 30% of them are in the U.S., and 10% are in China. 99.8% of these autos are internal combustion engine vehicles. TSE crew members need to work to get that percentage down to as low a double digit number as possible by 2030.

There are three new trends now unfolding that will greatly help us transform transportation.

Sharing economy

The first is the sharing economy manifested by such companies as Uber, Lyft, Zipcar Car2Go, and other such services around the world. Transportation when you need it, and only then. Why own a car in a city when there is always one available? This new sharing transportation economy is close to billions of uses to date, globally, as of this writing. Multiple uses by multiple people of a single car. This will lower emissions, lower the number of automobiles on streets and highways, and will therefore lessen the number of vehicles built and sold in the world, greatly reducing resource consumption.

If there are fewer cars in urban areas, there will be less congestion, which means less burning of fossil fuels, and lowering emissions. This phenomenon is in its earliest stage, so growth will be dramatic

Electric and hydrogen vehicles

In the years 2005–2015, the use of hybrids grew dramatically. It was also the beginning of the electric plug-in car industry. These cars burn no fossil fuels, except indirectly from the fossil fuel plants that generate the electricity that charges them. Increasingly, there will be closed looped systems where the electricity to power the plug-in vehicles will come from stored solar and wind energy. Though Tesla has rightly taken the brand and awareness lead, every single major automotive company is or will be producing electric plug-in vehicles. This will obviously extend to buses and trucks as costs come down, and the charging infrastructure scales up around the world.

Hydrogen fuel cell vehicles have already found their place in large distribution and manufacturing plants. Several automotive companies are in early stage production. This industry will take off by 2020, as the economies of scale on both the production and infrastructure sides occur, again, no carbon emissions as a result.

Autonomous automobiles

This is a game changer—the driverless car. A totally smart car that knows when it needs a recharge, and can always be moving people. Multiple people, even multiple families can use a single car. The average American uses their car less than 2 hours a day on average. If compatible families and work schedules can be matched, then the number of cars on highways around the world will decrease. The use and need of parking lots will decline. These heat-generating places could become urban gardens.

We are stuck with the entire car infrastructure. Our landscape has been shaped by the automobile, freeways, and on and off ramps while cities have been completely constructed around the assumed use of the personal car. Mall parking lots are scaled for Black Friday, what has traditionally been the largest shopping day of the Christmas season, the Friday after Thanksgiving. Ultimately, this will change over the next century, since we need to change rapidly. However, between 2015 and 2030, we have no choice except to make changes to this existing transport model that is in place. We make gas stations recharging stations; we insure that all big parking garages have charging stations and free temporary parking for autonomous automobiles.

The good news is that, at this moment, a number of global automobile brands are in various stages of development of autonomous automobiles. Early projections are that some 30% of all cars driven in the United States will be driverless by 2030. Crew consciousness can increase that percentage.

The sharing economy

The sharing economy, mentioned above, can play a big role in reducing emissions. The ever-expanding consumer economies around the world create too much stuff. People are provoked to buy more, or buy something that is new and shiny. As mentioned earlier in the book, waste does not go away, it just goes somewhere else on TSE. So, the less waste the better. When people use their cars 10% of the time, they own them. When people have second homes, they do not use them all the time. When people have extra room, stuff, vehicles, or anything that is under-utilized, sharing it and gaining revenue off an underutilized asset makes sense.

The sharing economy, as currently epitomized by AirBnb, Uber, or Lyft and other such sharing companies, actually makes great sense from a TSE point of view. The theoretical need to build ever more hotels or sell ever more cars that are underutilized can be mitigated by the sharing economy. Use what exists already. Don't buy it to sit idle, rent it when you need it. That makes great sense to TSE crew.

There is still some residual thinking in place that flowed from the planned obsolescence of the post-WWII consumer economies. The thinking that one has to buy a car every few years even if it has years of usage left, makes no sense. Through the lens of crew thinking, it makes no sense at all. Every time something is manufactured, some amount of planetary resource is used. The goal is to minimize such usage in order to get back to the 1.0 or < 1.0 resource footprint.

We can, therefore, add sharing to the reduce, reuse, recycle idea that is fundamental to TSE crew living.

Technology

This is one area where hope resides. We all know and have experienced how technology has transformed our lives. In just the last two decades, we have seen the arrival of the Internet and the mobile phone, which is now one of the greatest distributed computer powers, ever. Apps have changed how we interface with the world.

We are so connected that there is no longer any time, distance, or place limiting human connection. That could not be said ten years ago. This is creating a pulsating, synaptic, technologically connected consciousness that is becoming exponentially integrated. This means that TSE crew consciousness can spread more quickly than ever before.

3-D printing is here, and leading humanity into the next 21st century stage of production, and custom manufacturing. This will dramatically lower waste, and use lower levels of energy to produce.

Transportation of goods will drop as products can be produced much closer to the end user.

Nanotechnology, the production of almost anything in nanometers [a nanometer is one billionth of a meter], will transform medicine and many areas of industry.

Technology has reshaped much of our lives in the last 15 years, and this will continue at an accelerating pace, for the years leading up to 2030.

Here are some technologies, currently in the early stages of development that can, and will, help us as we attempt to lesser future catastrophes and disasters.

Atmospheric Cleansing

This is the game changer. It will bring us back into alignment on our way back down to 800 gigatonnes. As a species, we are great at putting greenhouse gases into the atmosphere. Now, we must develop technologies to remove them from the atmosphere. Fortunately, there is early stage development of such technologies. Chemicals, that when placed on the front side of wind turbine blades, capture CO_2 the wind is blowing. Titanium dioxide a whitening agent that, when painted on buildings, actually absorbs CO_2 from the immediate air surrounding the building.

However, most of these are technological expansion of the tree model. They are part of the solution and would help as we decrease emissions. We need to go far beyond the absorption model.

The transformative technology that might well come along within the next few years would go beyond the tree model and move to the "vacuum cleaner" model: actively sucking CO_2 particulates out of the atmosphere. This is an environmentalist's holy grail technology.

—David Houle
    from "Entering the Shift Age" (2013)

This will happen quickly as we now know we have a problem. The Silicon Valleys and other communities of innovation will deploy to create such technologies. It will happen, as those that create such cleansing technology will become billionaires. Saving humanity and thousands of other species, preventing trillions of dollars of losses, saving tens of millions of lives will all create incredible value. The hope here is that with focus, ample investment, and multiple design visions, this technology can be installed and can be rapidly scaled in the 2020s, the decade when we will really see the need for them.

A locally placed, moveable tower that will clean air in its immediate area is now in early stage of funding and development. This is an early stage example of what local neighborhoods can do to both clean up the air that they breathe and, when scaled, will capture CO_2 to a measurable amount. This is a scaled up version of the air purifiers we have in our homes.

There will be larger, more industrial strength and sized, inventions that will actively remove CO_2 and other greenhouse gas emissions from the atmosphere. We imagine that they will be both on the ground to capture from the surrounding areas, and high up in the atmosphere, perhaps with balloons. There might be some ionic or catalytic technology.

The need for atmospheric cleansing technologies is great. The cost ratio to build versus long-term catastrophic costs will be good. The amount of wealth created for the inventors and builders of such technologies will be enormous. The growing TSE crew consciousness will drive inventors, Venture Capital funds, and entrepreneurs to create these technologies. The hope is that these technologies will come into use before 2020.

If we are so good at putting greenhouse gases into the atmosphere, we should be able to develop the technologies to remove them.

These are just some of the major initiatives humanity must undertake, and aggressively expand by 2030. TSE crew consciousness will deepen and expand the thinking in this chapter. We just wanted to suggest some of the major changes in thinking that must be done. The ideas in this chapter are the big ones that cities, countries, governments, industry, and entrepreneurs must undertake collectively and scale up as soon as possible.

We now look at what individuals can do to start living a TSE crew conscious life.

Chapter 9

WHAT CAN I DO?

I want to help, but I don't know what to do.

—Ron Zeitler

Many people look at the world around them and are disturbed by what they see, read, and experience. For some, the trigger is smog and air quality, for others it is litter. Then, there are the beach closures due to high bacterial counts, the food recalls due to a range of contaminants, and growing concerns over water quality, quantity, and availability. Still others find themselves in a general malaise about the future when considering the status of TSE. This is played forward with the needs of another billion and half people being added to the mix. They know things have to change, but where does one begin?

> *Destiny is not a matter of chance; it is a*
> *matter of choice: it is not a thing to be*
> *waited for; it is a thing to be achieved.*

—William Jennings Bryant

Looking at the scale of the issues that have been presented in this book, it would be easy to become overwhelmed and assume that nothing can change, nothing will change, and what any of us does would not have an impact.

> *Think that you are too small to make a*
> *difference? Try spending the night with*
> *a mosquito.*

—The Dali Lama

This is where being crew on TSE makes the difference. There are dozens, if not hundreds to thousands, of things we can do. Some are so small as to seem insignificant; others will at first seem habits too difficult to break. Realistically, all are doable. They all matter, and add up. As crew, we know we are not alone or isolated in the process. We do not have to change the world by ourselves. We do not have to resolve every issue on our own. We are crew—we are in this together—we have a common goal. Nobody is asking or expecting, anybody—much less everybody—to do everything or to be perfect. The need is for each of us to do our part. Ecosystems thrive on the interactions and interdependencies of diversity. Each organism does its part in the context of its physical environment, and in concert with the organisms comprising the system. It is the same with humanity. We engage, do our best, and the cumulative, collective, continuous impact of our combined actions changes the entire outcome.

It was the cumulative, collective, and continuous impact of our unawareness and insular approach to events that brought us to the current condition of TSE. It is the cumulative, collective, and continuous impact that our actions, in the context of a systems-based, holistic approach to our relationship with TSE, give a viable and verdant future.

> *Saving civilization is not a spectator sport.*
> *We all have to get involved.*
>
> —Lester Brown

Primum non nocere and noblesse oblige

If there were themes or guidelines for moving forward, they would probably align with these DO ideals:

DO Ideals	
Primum non nocere	Noblesse oblige
Above all, do no harm	Nobility obligates

First, do no harm, seems like the logical place to start. While ultimately it is, and should be the starting point, unfortunately it is a somewhat distant goal. Doing harm is the current status quo. In a consumption-based economic model, creating waste is automatic. Add to that an accounting methodology that excludes environmental costs, ignores social worth, while incorporating a profit model that supports, encourages, and frequently depends upon negative externalities, and the result is, we end up where we are.

Pollution is an externality. An externality is the impact on a third party that was not directly involved in the financial transaction. In its 2015

State of the Air Report, the American Lung Association stated that, "Nearly 138.5 million people—almost 44 percent of the nation—live where pollution levels are too often dangerous to breathe," and "Nearly 24 million people in the United States live in counties with unhealthful year-round levels of particle pollution." Those are citizens living in and breathing an externality.

> *If you do not change direction, you may*
> *end up where you are heading.*
>
> —Lao Tzu

KMPG, one of the world's largest accounting/audit companies, estimated that in 2008 the 3,000 largest public companies were estimated to be causing $2.15 trillion (USD) of environmental damage. In a separate calculation, KPMG estimated that it would cost corporations 41 cents of each dollar of revenue if those corporations had to pay for the services that nature provides.

> *In Nature's economy the currency is not*
> *money, it is life.*
>
> —Vandana Shiva

To achieve *primum non nocere*, we need to support those companies and entities that currently integrate environmental, social, and economic costs in the proper way and disincentivize those corporations that do not. The economy is set in a social framework that is dependent upon a healthy and fully functioning environment. The metaphor of the three-legged stool for sustainability is wrong, as the so-called legs are not of equivalent value and function for the long-term viability of humanity on TSE. The environment is not dependent upon the economy, but the economy is dependent upon the environment.

> *The conservation of natural resources*
> *is the fundamental problem. Unless we*
> *solve that problem it will avail us little to*
> *solve all others.*
>
> —President Theodore Roosevelt

As to *noblesse oblige*, this is an issue of fairness. Those who know more, and/or have the power or influence to assist should and must do more.

Fairness is not an issue of body count but of capability. And *doing* is the measure. It is not enough to know what could be done and operate under the assumption that because the information exists, that the other guy will do the right thing. Just as we all live down-wind and down-stream from someone, we are each the other guy's, other guy. Everything we do impacts TSE. There are no neutral acts. The environment responds to what we do, not what we think, or how we feel. In that respect, TSE is very Newtonian. Every action triggers a reaction. And, the combination of those events and the chain reaction they generate are either to the net benefit of TSE or to its net harm. While we can find examples that would suggest we are on a path of improved prosperity for some portion of our species, at present our net effect on TSE and the future of our species is on the negative side of the ledger.

> *Our inventions are wont to be pretty toys,*
> *which distract our attention from serious*
> *things. They are but improved means to an*
> *unimproved end.*
>
> —Henry David Thoreau

Putting ourselves in TSE context

> *No matter how far you have gone on the*
> *wrong road, turn back.*
>
> —Turkish Proverb

Part of the change we need to make is contextual. We need to see ourselves as crew and act accordingly by developing crew consciousness and keeping in mind that TSE is the only place in the universe with an environment complimentary to our continuation, as we naturally exist. Functionally, we need to be more curious, more thorough, more thoughtful, and more responsible. We need to ask better and bigger questions rather than looking for a right answer to a poor question.

Full and best use

Do we want a paper or a plastic bag at the grocery store is a great example of a poor question. The more fundamental question is what are we going to do with the bag. Do we have a known and intended next use for either type of bag? A more responsible approach to the issue would focus on the fact that we knew we were going to the grocery store, we knew we were going to buy things, we knew we were going to need a bag, so why did we make the less than responsible choice of not bringing a bag? If we do not have a way to use the bag for its physical lifetime, or a way to safely and functional repurpose the bag of choice, then all we have done is transported our groceries home by causing future harm to TSE.

What happens to the plastic bag? In 2010, the US only managed to recycle 0.6% of the 100 BILLION plastic bags that were used that year. The plastic bag does not biodegrade, but does physically break down. The breakdown process takes at least 10 years. It is a mismatch of time on task, and duration of material to use a plastic bag to bring home groceries. Do any of us have a ten-year plan for plastic bags from the store? Even after the 10 years, the plastic is still active in the biological and physical environment.

The paper bag is not an environmental freebie either. In fact, nothing is an environmental freebie. Paper bags require more energy and water to make than plastic bags. Paper bags add more pollutants to water than do plastic bags. Given that paper bags weigh more than plastic bags, their transportation impacts are greater, and they take up more space in a landfill.

Both types of bags need natural resources in their generation, and while paper bags have the potential to be compostable, most landfill designs do not promote sufficient oxygen circulation to provide the appropriate conditions for composting. As a result, both types of bags functionally end up being stored or warehoused in landfills for a prolonged time.

When we fall into the mental trap of paper or plastic while in the check-out line, we think we are making a good decision. In reality, we are selecting what we believe is the less bad choice. Crew members bring their own bags.

What then, are the minimum requirements
for living organisms? First, we certainly
need growth, if only as a necessary prelude
to replication. This implies that there is
available a source of free energy (in the

thermodynamic sense)—in the last analysis
this is provided by sunlight. The organism
must be an "open system" into which
chemicals flow and from which chemicals
flow out again, so that it can obtain both the
atoms and the energy needed for synthesis.
The organism must be able to metabolize,
using raw materials for its own synthetic
ends, so that it can build up the molecules
it needs in order to maintain itself and
reproduce in a hostile world.

—William McDonough

Paradigms

How do we assess information? How do we make sense of the world? In the course of a day, we are all exposed to differing thoughts, information, and stimuli. We put those things through our own mental sorting process. Some of the information we will keep and use, some of it we will share, some we will disregard, and others we will argue against. There may be pieces that we find humorous, some will be sad, and some will shock us either for their audacity or stupidity. How we select which pieces go where, is our paradigm. It has been established by what we have seen, and lived through. It has been impacted by our value and belief systems. It has been shaped by what we have been taught and learned, as well as all the things that were left out of, or diminished by, our education. We do not know the importance of questions we were taught to ignore, or the value of information we do not have.

Our educational institutions need to see
their purpose not as training personnel
for exploiting the earth but as guiding
students toward an intimate relationship
with the earth.

—Thomas Berry

Cognitive symbiosis, not willful ignorance

For the past 70+ years, we have been relatively accepting and passive consumers in the market place. We have been rather laissez-faire in our interactions with, and responsibilities to, the environment as well as the future welfare of humanity. On the whole, we have done a poor job of asking questions, verifying assumptions over the long-term, and being accountable for the conditions we have generated on TSE. At times, it seems we have merged the idiom of ignorance is bliss, with Joseph Campbell's very different implication of "follow your bliss," and have decided to follow our ignorance.

> *The error of the past is the wisdom of the future.*
>
> —Dale Turner

In developing crew consciousness, each of us should examine our own paradigm, and see how well it matches with the reality of TSE. Where necessary, we should shift our paradigm to promote the cognitive symbiosis of humanity and TSE. Do our words match our actions, and do our actions help generate a future in balance with TSE? There should be absolutely no need for a crew to come in and clean up after an Earth Day celebration. If there is a need for a sanitation crew, then Earth was not celebrated.

Perspectives

We should each examine our perspectives. Do we see ourselves as part of a community? Do we see ourselves as part of a continuum? Do we see where we fit in the story of TSE, and do we see where we fit in improving the relationship of humanity with TSE? Do we believe that everything is connected to everything else?

> *When we rise in the morning... at the table we drink coffee form which is provided us by a South American, or tea by a Chinese, or cocoa by a west African. Before we leave for our jobs we are already beholden to more than half the world.*
>
> —Dr. Martin Luther King

We are caught in an inescapable network
of mutuality tied in a single garment of
destiny, whatever affects one directly
affects all indirectly."

—Dr. Martin Luther King
Letter from a Birmingham jail

Have we considered all people that we have not met, for whom we are dependent? How many of us get to do what we do because we can afford not to grow our own food, make our own clothes, spend the day hauling water, or look for material that we can burn for warmth and cooking? How many of us think about the individuals making the microchips and writing the software upon which we depend? Out of sight can no longer be out of consciousness on TSE.

So where do we begin?

Do what you can, with what you have,
where you are.

—Theodore Roosevelt

We begin at home.

Can we reduce the amount of waste we generate? That is, all kinds of waste—solid waste, energy waste, and water waste.

<u>Energy waste</u>

Many electronic devices, like phone chargers, computer chargers, coffee makers and cable boxes operate in a standby mode. That is to say, they are always on to some degree waiting for the signal from the remote, to have the device plugged back into the charger, or maintaining the status of the fully charged device to which they are still connected. On an individual basis, one might try to argue that the energy use of any one of those devices is very small. While one might appreciate that position, crew members understand that we actually live on a TSE basis. In the average American home, the energy vampires of stand-by mode generate approximately 10% of the monthly energy bill. The issue is not simply the 10%, it is the waste of all the time, effort, energy, materials and resources that created the energy that you did not need to use, as well as the pollution generated by all the related activities to get that energy to your home.

Food Waste

From time to time, we clean out the refrigerator and the pantry shelves. There are the leftovers that were left too long. The apples that one never quite got around to eating, as well as the chips that went stale. On average, Americans toss out a little over a pound of food per person per day. When you also include the water, energy fertilizers, and other factors involved in growing the wasted food, the economic value of food waste is about $165 billion dollars a year in the USA, and $1 trillion dollars (USD) world wide. In a country, and in a world of hungry people, we are currently throwing away 25% of the food calories available for consumption. The issue has become such a concern that the US government, in partnership with other organizations and corporations, has initiated a challenge to reduce food waste by 50% by 2030.

Living in TSE consciousness

Live in TSE consciousness by being smarter and doing better. Buy local, support locally owned businesses, purchase what you are going to use, and avoid stuff for the sake of stuff. Reduce your use of plastic. Promote buying products that are created from disassembling and reusing material diverted from the waste stream. Living in TSE consciousness is not about compromising or lowering your quality of life. It is about doing a better job of matching resource use with human need in the context of TSE's life support system.

Healthy environments do not generate either pollution or garbage and trash. Currently, humanity does both. We do not have to, but we choose to do so. Now, we have reached a time and condition in which we must choose not to do so for the health and benefit currently on board TSE, and for those we envision replacing us.

Where do you fit in the story and the solution?

Everything we do, every action we take, either improves the environment for humanity on TSE, or diminishes the quality of life of our species' future. The effect of each of those actions is multiplied by the number of crew members who engage as well as the number of passengers who disengage.

> *Unus pro omnibus, omnes pro uno* One for all, all for one

> —Alexandre Dumas
> The Three Musketeers

Things you can do to promote the vitality of TSE and TSE consciousness

This is not a full and exhaustive list of all that we can do, but it is a start. More examples can be found on the website—and you can send us examples and suggestions.

Keep in mind that no one expects anyone to do everything that is on this list or its continuing iterations. For a variety of age-related, economic, legal, social, and cultural reasons, there are likely to be things that are out of reach or non-permissible. What is expected of every crew member is that they will find the events they can do, and will then do them.

The universal things

- Be curious.
- Be engaged.
- Be proactive.
- Be responsible.
- Support the future.
- Check the backstory–confirm/validate your assumptions about what you buy, use, consume, and throw away.
- Do your choices match your morals, ethics, and the Golden Rule?
- Increase your support in and use of those things that are good for TSE.
- Decrease, limit, stop your support, and use of things harmful to TSE and living things.

These considerations are being suggested due to the number of industrially produced chemicals that humans are exposed to on a daily and on-going basis. The EPA lists 86,000 chemicals used in commercial and consumer products. Most of these chemicals have not been specifically tested regarding human safety. Then the question becomes, whether the testing done appropriately reflects the cumulative exposure pattern of the consumer. For example, a 2009 study by the Environmental Working Group found an average of 232 chemicals in the cord blood of 10 babies.

What you eat

- Eat local
- Eat seasonal
- Eat Fresh
- Eat organic (this is about soil and TSE health)
- Eat humane (this is about animal welfare)

Know the source of your food

The bar code on the food can give you the country of origin, and this will provide an idea of shipping implications. More importantly, it may imply what pesticide/ chemicals rules were used to establish the health and safety of your upcoming meal. In Japan, the QR code tag on the food allows you to know the originating farm of your food. Petition your favorite market and political leaders to allow you to have access to the same information.

Know your seafood

Was your seafood pole caught—that is to say each fish was caught individually to reduce bycatch (the fish caught, harmed, killed, and then dumped overboard, because the fishing technique used was not specific to the fish species destined for the market).

Is the species population of the seafood you are eating regarded as fully exploited or over exploited? Is the seafood species being managed in a sustainable manner? And, is the seafood listed on the menu or the package, actually the seafood you are eating. Recent DNA studies indicated that over 30% of the fish tested were not the species that were being marketed.

Buying food

- Support urban agriculture.
- Support real farmer's markets.
- Support aquaponics, hydroponics, aquaculture that support TSE
- Support regenerative farming.
- Support heirloom foods.
- Support heritage livestock.
- Support integrated farming.
- Support vertical agriculture and indoor agriculture.
- Support rooftop farming.
- Support local grocery stores.
- Join a CSA (Community Supported Agriculture) where you buy shares of the harvest in advance, which reduces the debt load on the farm and farmer.
- Encourage your favorite take-out/take-way place to use compostable and/or recyclable containers–not Styrofoam-type packaging.

Around the house

- Have a used/usable landscape.
  Avoid lawn for the sake of lawn. The volume of chemicals and water needed to keep a lawn as a lawn are significant, especially if you are not going to actively engage in the space. As you wander and travel, how many people do you actually see using the front yard? Why expend the resources to maintain an empty place? When did wildflowers and butterflies become ugly? When did a meadow become something that should be mowed out of existence?
- Foodscape your land.
  Grow edibles, herbs, and culturally important plants.
- Dye/fiber-scape your land.
  Grow plants that you can use.
- Habiscape your land.
  Create native habitat for flowers, songbirds, butterflies, frogs, etc.
- Permaculture your land.
  Grow green space, a grassy area that you are going to USE.
- Be rain-wise, catch it for use, and keep it on your property via a swale; do not make storm water and runoff.

What you drink

- No more disposable bottled water.
  Get a reusable water bottle and refill it as needed. In the US, we throw away 2.5 million plastic bottles an hour. So, no more plastic bottles. A recent study found that on college campuses when plastic water bottles sales were halted, that it did not reduce the amount of plastic bottles being trashed. People simply switched to other liquids in plastic bottles.
- When it comes to coffee, tea, and coco, support Fair Trade, Shade Grown, Rainforest, Alliance Certified, Bird Friendly, Organic and Child-Labor Free brands and blends. Ask the barista about the origin of the drink you are about to order; make it clear that future purchases depend upon the company doing right by TSE, and the individuals who provide the product you are about to order.

Transportation

- Reduce the amount of time you are the single occupant in the car being used.
- Reduce the amount of time you are using a car.
- Plan your route to minimizing back tracking and traffic congestion.
- Bike when you can.
- Walk when you can.
- Promote Shade or other culturally and environmentally appropriate coverings so that the walk is not something to be endured but enjoyed.
- Use public transportation when you can.
- Lobby for effective public transportation.
  Effective involves frequency, consistency, predictability of pick up times, efficient transfer options, safe and weather appropriate waiting stations at transport stops, as well as well maintained and fuel appropriate vehicles.

Clothing and personal care products

- Go with natural fiber materials whenever possible.
  A 2011 report, indicated that synthetic material shed an average of 1900 micro plastic pieces each time it was laundered in a washing machine. Those micro-plastics are too small to be captured in the

water treatment process, and are released into the aquatic environment where they can be, and are, consumed by fish.

- Avoid personal care products with micro-beads as those also end up in the aquatic environment at a rate of 8,000,000,000,000 a day in the US.
- Research the chemicals in the personal care products you use. Some can act as hormone mimics affecting gender development.
- Research the chemicals in the make-up you use, as they can contain lead, mercury, and other toxic materials.

Energy use

- Turn things off, as in off, not stand-by mode, but off at the plug so that the appliances are not using energy except when they are in active use.
- Support alternative energy, especially solar and wind, as they do not require a continuous water supply for the generation of energy. Given the need for water for humanity, business, manufacturing, and agriculture, do we really want to continue the expansion of water competition.
- Support the change from generation and transfer of energy (which is very inefficient) to capture and storage of energy at the point of use.
- Support non-polluting energy systems. There are currently power plants in the US that are polluting, but connecting them to an algae farm would zero the power plants pollution while creating another marketable product that could be used as fuel, animal feed, a substitute for plastic, or a food supplement.
- Reduce your energy demand by switching to CFL or LED lighting, upgrading your home's insulation, and upgrading to more energy efficiency appliances when replacing lost of damaged products.
- Depending upon your geographic and climate region, adopt the most appropriate shading and wind break vegetation for the area around your home, as well as the most climate appropriate color and materials for the home to either reduce heat loading or improve heat capture depending upon average annual need.

Public actions one can take–in the philosophy of *primum non nocere*

- Leave the packaging at the store. Some of the items we buy are over packaged in plastic. Once you have purchased the item, field strip the packaging, and put in the trash receptacle at the store. Make the cost of disposal, the stores responsibility. If enough crew members follow suit, the stores will encourage suppliers and security systems that are not waste stream heavy.

- Say thank you. When you find a company or store making TSE improvements in its service and operations, let them know that you, a customer, appreciate their efforts.

- Ask Questions. At the locations you work, shop, and frequent, ask if they are a green business, or if you can, have a copy of their sustainability plan In a few weeks ask again, and then again until the enterprise understands the value of having a TSE answer to the question. If they don't change their ways, change where you frequent.

- Ask questions of any person running for office or in office what they are willing or will be doing, and what issues they will or will not advocate to improve our relationship with TSE. Make it clear that your vote is dependent on what they say and do.

- Create competition between neighborhoods, towns, cities, and states, schools, colleges, on water usage, energy usage, carbon footprint, and amount of waste.

- Practice Guerrilla Gardening. Plant gardens (native plants or food) to care for neglected public spaces. Add beauty, habitat, and sustenance to your community. Plant trees wherever you can legally do so.

- Reverse Graffiti. Find dirty walls or facades and ERASE/CLEAN the dirt to create an image or graphic or other appropriate TSE messages (i.e. "Are you a TSE crew member?" "A solar panel on every rooftop!" "Plant a tree." "Climate Change will be the largest catastrophe your children will have to face." "What are you doing?") Come up with your own. Remember, changing consciousness is the goal. Worse case scenario for the art is that to remove it, all the city has to do is wash a wall it should have already cleaned up.

- Signage for Understanding. Who are the trees and plants that share your neighborhood? Identify the trees and label them—who are they, who is native, and who is introduced and/or invasive. What wildlife uses the tree? Along a similar vein, use the signage to show the watershed you live in, or to identify the crops you drive by. Create some aesthetic signage to inform your neighbors. One cannot use information they do not have or care for things they do not know or understand. Provide some insights.

- Chalk for TSE. While similar to the action above, the difference is that this one is temporary and of the moment. It can be a simple list—birds seen today. It can be a reminder of the full moon or a meteor shower, or of world water day. It can be an interesting fact—daily average water use for your community, gallons of rainfall, or the average amount of trash disposed of per week, or the travel distance of the average carrot in a store near you. These are thought triggers, a kind of *did you know*, and then letting the individual reader of the chalk reflect upon the information and take their own action.

- Collaborative Ventures for TSE. What are some public and positive things that a group of you can do or organize? Litter pick-up–with a local station sharing the results with the community? Conduct a removal of exotic and invasive species with permission of the landowners? Can you provide speakers for discussion groups on local, regional, national, international TSE issues? Functionally, you are creating invitations for individuals to switch from Team Passenger to Team TSE.

- Use activism to be heard. Be loud and clear that you will only vote for candidates that will accept Climate Change as the major issue of our times.

- Vote against anyone who does not demonstrate and communicate that you have become TSE crew and help others to become crew as well.

- Work with those that want institutions and investment funds to divest their holdings of all carbon oriented companies. Crew consciousness will make fossil fuel companies short-term investments anyway, so time to divest.

- Actively support any company or individuals working to increase the use of renewable energies.

- Every day work to decrease your carbon footprint. Help others to do so as well.

Chapter 10

METAMORPHOSIS AND
A CALL TO ACTION

Our challenge is perhaps the largest collective challenge in our species' history. The last time there was the same amount of Resident CO_2 in the atmosphere, as there is today, was 800,000 years ago. Modern Humanity has been around for 200,000, so the conditions we are creating is something our species has never experienced. There are no reference points from our past to guide us.

> ...*he not busy being born is busy dying*
> —Bob Dylan

We have two choices. We can change our thinking and actions in ways that are unprecedented and create a solution from our collective consciousness. Or, we can continue along the path of the ways things are, and steal the quality of life from our children, and the few future generations that will occur. Either way, the decision is now a conscious choice.

It seems that a general concern regarding change is—what we will have to give up. We want to know if we will have to leave our comfort zone. We have doubts as to whether or not the changes will really have a benefit. We, also, can more clearly imagine the way things can go wrong, rather than being able to envision the benefits of a future with which we have no experience.

For the past several decades, we have "believed" that increasing economic prosperity and improving the quality of life were the same path, or at least intertwined. We have now arrived at a transformational moment. What has made us most comfortable, and what is most conducive to our survival on TSE, are not in the same paradigm.

It's not working

It's not working has almost become the mantra of the global perspective.

It is certainly a common refrain in news stories about politics and the economy. The various attempts to stimulate economies are not generating the intended results. Political parties seem to be more fractious and more interested in promoting a narrow, party-specific policy than in compromising for the benefit of all.

Then, there is the weather/climate that does not seem to be working to our liking, and even rebellions are not working as an expected mechanism of change. Every which way we turn, progress at the community, city, national, or global scale seems to have hit the wall. As we try to overcome the various scenarios by expanding the use of our tried and true methodologies, we do not get the changes we seek and the frustration grows. So, our thinking simply has to change.

> *Think Different*
> —Steve Jobs

Re-conceptualizing processes

Complex systems grow to a certain scale, at which time they need to restructure, redesign, and redevelop themselves to maintain and maximize efficiency and effectiveness. We are at that stage, and now is that time.

The survival crisis humanity has entered is one of our own construction and creation. It is the result of silo thinking and linear processes. It is the logical consequence of a growth model based on the assumption of disconnected parts, and unlimited resources. We are all part of a single system, a planetary system. We readily accept that we are ever more connected, and collective technologically—we need to adopt that same acceptance relative to the planetary reality of TSE.

TSE consciousness

We need to promote the cooperative model inherent in systems design. Nature does this all the time. At its heart, ecological systems are cooperative models. If you are a pro-silo thinker, then your tendency might well be to focus your perspective on a single aspect of an eco-system. That could be predator-prey; it could be population size of grazing animals; or, it could be migration cycles just to name a few options.

However, looking at the parts of a system out of context, and in isolation, can lead one to false conclusions about future events. This thinking never lets one see, or comprehend the benefits of the synergy of the whole. TSE consciousness is about supporting the synergy of the whole.

In practical terms—

Will one still be able to have a house—Yes?

Will one still be able to have individual transportation—Yes?

But, it will be different; it will all be different.

Our home will not be dependent upon the electrical grid or a centralized water system. It will partner with them. Our home will capture, store, and share energy—it won't just use energy. Our home will capture rainwater, and it will sequence water use to match need, as well as water quality to the task. It won't just take water and generate polluted water. Instead, the return water will go through a treatment train—a series of linked and sequenced water purification systems to maximize the efficiency and effectiveness of water use, while simultaneously reducing water demand.

Our transportation system will be multimodal. It will be by vehicle, by public transit, by bike, by foot and by a wide range of additional devices—and none of it will be based on the internal combustion engine. Cities and communities will be (re)designed to utilize multiple means of transportation so that the convenience factor of transportation will not be lost—only its exhaust.

We will be able to accomplish everything we do now, but we will do it differently. With two major exceptions:

- We will not generate waste, and
- we will not pollute.

Instead, we will use services and create assets—that is the synergy of the system.

Instead of using the buried treasure savings account of fossil fuels, we can live off our income of solar, wind, and other alternative and renewable energy sources. The amount of sunlight that hits TSE every hour can supply all the energy TSE crew needs for a day. So, in a radically different, retrofitted TSE, we can actually create extra energy, every day. Our daily energy income can be greater than our use of it; we can accumulate unused energy, every day, and not release any emissions at all.

No Silver Bullet

There is no silver bullet, no one-size-fits-all solution to the issues we face. Nor, is there a magic wand wizard, which spells instantaneous resolution to the problems before us. But, there are so many solutions already available that work in different places, and at different scales with many creative and industrious individuals amongst the current and the soon-to-be crew. The Life Support System of TSE can be knit whole, again, in this century.

It starts with a change of consciousness. We have to individually, and collectively move from uninformed and/or disconnected passengers to engaged and conscientious crew. This is the time that anybody who ever wanted to be an astronaut can be. All it takes is to realize that you already are one.

We urgently appeal to you to become crew and develop crew consciousness. Remember, that you—and the rest of us—are dependent upon recirculating resources on a finite TSE. Meeting our needs will become visible and predominate when we act from that new understanding, and the alternative ways of having meaningful lives.

We have made clear that humanity's window of proactivity is 2015–2030. We have given ourselves a time frame—by being disengaged, unaware, reluctant, or recalcitrant passengers on a hypothetical Cruise ship Earth. For too long, we have acted as if our relationship with TSE was unilateral—that TSE was here to serve us and there was no need for reciprocity. Now, we understand that we are in a partnership with TSE, and, collectively, we need to embrace the responsibility of crew consciousness as fast as possible. Currently, there are openings for over 7 billion volunteers.

You now know that you are part of the story—that you are cause and effect, as well as detriment or solution. So, what are you going to do now that you know?

Will you become crew? Will you recruit other crewmembers?

The future of civilization as we know it, is more at risk every day that we hold onto and promote our passenger status. The future is in our hands.

What are we going to do?

What are you going to do?

Be the change. Become crew. Help others become shipmates of TSE.

Then take actions.

Please!

Thank you for reading this book. Please feel free to share the book and its concepts with someone else, so they might become crew as well.

References

Chapter 1

Anders, William A. *Earthrise.* 1968. NASA. NASA.gov. Web. 11 October 2015.

"Crew." Def. 2. *Merriam-webster Online.* N.p., n.d. Web. 10 Oct. 2015.
    <http://www.merriam-webster.com/dictionary/crew.>

Fuller, R. Buckminster. *Operating Manual for Spaceship Earth.* Carbondale: Southern Illinois University
    Press, 1969. Print.

Houle, David. *Entering the Shift Age: The End of the Information Age and the New Era of Transformation.*
    Naperville: Sourcebooks, 2012. Print.

Houle, David. *The Shift Age.* N.p. 2007. Print.

"In 2015, Earth Overshoot Day lands on August 13." *Earth Overshoot Day 2015,* 2015. Web. 20 November
    2015. Web.
    <http://www.overshootday.org>

McLam, Eric. "The ecological impact of the Industrial Revolution." *Ecology.com,* 2006. Web. 6 June 2015.
    <http://www.ecology.com/2011/09/18/ecological-impact-industrial-revolution/>

"Passenger." Def. 1. *Merriam-webster Online.* N.p., n.d. Web. 10 Oct. 2015.
    <http://www.merriam-webster.com/dictionary/passenger.>

"Current World Population." *Worldometers,* 2015. Web. 20 November 2015.
    <http://www.worldometers.info/world-population/>

Rosenberg, Matt. "Current world population." *About education,* n.d. Web. 20 November 2015.
    <http://geography.about.com/od/obtainpopulationdata/a/worldpopulation.htm>

"World footprint, do we fit on the planet?" Global Footprint Network. World Footprint, 20 November 2015.
    Web. 23 November 2015.
    <http://www.footprintnetwork.org/en/index.php/GFN/page/world_footprint>

Chapter 2

"7 million premature deaths annually linked to air pollution." Media Centre. *World Health Organization,* 25
    March 2014. Web. 14 July 2015. <http://www.who.int/mediacentre/news/releases/2014/air-pollution/en/>

Alkire, MD, Blake C., Raykar, MD, Nakul P., Shrime, MD, Mark G., Weiser, MD, Thomas G., Bickler, MD,
    Prof Stephen W., Rose, MD, John A., Nutt, BA, Cameron T., Greenberg, MD, Sarah L.M., Kotagai,
    MD, Meera, Riesel, Johanna N., Esquivel, MD, Micaela, Uribe-Leitz, MD, Tarsicio, Molina, MD,
    George, Roy, MD, Prof Nobhojit, Meara, MD, John G., Farmer, MD, Prof Paul E. "Global access to
    surgical care: a modelling study." *The Lancet Global Health.* Volume 3, No. 6 e316-e323. DOI: http://
    dx.doi.org/10.1016/S2214-109X(15)70115-4, 26 April 2015. Web. 14 July 2015.
    <http://www.thelancet.com/journals/langlo/article/PIIS2214-109X(15)70115-4/abstract>

"Ban on microbeads offers best chance to protect oceans, aquatic species." Phys.org, 16 September 2015. Web. 24 November 2015. <http://phys.org/news/2015-09-microbeads-chance-oceans-aquatic-species.html>

Ceballos, Gerardo., Ehrlich, Paul R., Barnosky, Anthony D., García, André, Pringle, Robert M., Palmer, Todd M. "Accelerated modern human–induced species losses: Entering the sixth mass extinction." Science Advances, Vol. 1. no. 5. e1400253. DOI: 10.1126/sciadv.1400253, 22 October 2015. Web. 27 October 2015. <http://advances.sciencemag.org/content/1/5/e1400253>

"Childhood overweight and obesity." Global Strategy on Diet, Physical Activity and Health. World Health Organization, n.d. Web. 20 November 2015. <http://www.who.int/dietphysicalactivity/childhood/en/>

"Current World Population." Worldometers, 2015. Web. 20 November 2015. <http://www.worldometers.info/world-population>

"Desertification—environmental degredation." World Day to Combat Desertification. United Nations,17 June 2015. Web. 20 November 2015. <http://www.un.org/en/events/desertificationday/background.shtml>

Diaz, B., Rosenberg, R. "Dead zones." VIMS. Virgina Institute of Marine Science, n.d. Web. 22 October 2015. <http://www.vims.edu/research/topics/dead_zones/index.php>

Eilperin, Juliet. "World's Fish Supply Running Out, Researchers Warn." The Washington Post, 3 November 2006. Web. 21 October 2015. <http://www.washingtonpost.com/wp-dyn/content/article/2006/11/02/AR2006110200913.html>

"Environmental risk." The world health report, Chapter 4. World Health Organization, 15 August 2013. Web. 20 November 2015. <http://www.who.int/whr/2002/chapter4/en/index7.html>

Fischer, E.M., Knutti, R. "Anthropogenic contribution to global occurrence of heavy-precipitation and high-temperature extremes." Nature Climate Change, 5, 560–564 (2015) doi:10.1038/nclimate2617 Received 27 November 2014. Web. 21 October 2015. <http://www.nature.com/nclimate/journal/v5/n6/full/nclimate2617.html>

Frankel, Todd,C. "New NASA data show how the world is running out of water." The Washington Post, 16 June 2016. Web. 22 October 2015. <http://www.washingtonpost.com/news/wonkblog/wp/2015/06/16/new-nasa-studies-show-how-the-world-is-running-out-of-water/>

Frutos, V., González-Comadrán, M., Solà, I., Jacquemin, B., Carreras, R. Vizcaíno, MA, Checa. "Impact of air pollution on fertility: a systematic review." US National Library of Medicine, National Institutes of Health, Gynecol Endocrinol.2015 Jan;31(1):7-13, epub 2014 Sep 12. Web 11 November 2015. <http://www.ncbi.nlm.nih.gov/pubmed/25212280>

Ghosj, JK, Heck, J.E., Cockburn, M. Su, J. Jerrett, M. Ritz, B. "Prenatal exposure to traffic-related air pollution and risk of early childhood cancers." Am J Epidemiol. US National Library of Medicine, National Institutes of Health, 2013 Oct 15;178(8):1233-9, epub 2013 Aug 28. Web. 19 November 2015. <http://www.ncbi.nlm.nih.gov/pubmed/23989198>

"Global Burden of Disease Due to Asthma." The Global Asthma Report, 2014. Web. 19 November 2015. <http://www.globalasthmareport.org/burden/burden.php>

"Global WASH Fast Facts." Global Water, Sanitation, & Hygiene (WASH). *Centers for Disease Control and Prevention (CDC)*, 5 June 2015. Web. 14 July 2015.
<http://www.cdc.gov/healthywater/global/wash_statistics.html>

"Great Pacific Garbage Patch." *National Geographic, Education*, n.d. Web. 19 November 2015.
<http://education.nationalgeographic.com/encyclopedia/great-pacific-garbage-patch/>

Greenberg, Neil (ed.). "Captain Charles Moore." *Earth Island Journal*, Spring 2009. Web. 19 November 2015.
<http://www.earthisland.org/journal/index.php/eij/article/charles_moore/>

Hooke, Roger LeB. and José F. Martín-Duque. "Land transformation by humans: A review." *GSA Today*. The Geological Society of America–*GSA TODAY*, Vol. 22 Issue 12 (December 2012), 4-10. Web. 19 November 2015. <http://www.geosociety.org/gsatoday/archive/22/12/article/i1052-5173-22-12-4.htm>

Hoornweg, D. Bhada-Tata, P., Kennedy, C. "Environment: waste production must peak this century." *Nature*, 30 October 2015. Web. 22 October 2013.
<http://www.nature.com/news/environment-waste-production-must-peak-this-century-1.14032>

"How much water is there on, in and above the Earth?" *The USGS Water Science School. United States Geological Survey*, 6 November 2015. Web. 19 November 2015.
<http://water.usgs.gov/edu/earthhowmuch.html>

"Increase of air pollution." *Max-Planck-Gesellschaft*, 1 August 2012. Web. 19 November 2015.
<https://www.mpg.de/5928050/global_air-pollution>

"Is sea level rising?" *National Ocean Service. National Oceanic and Atmospheric Administration*, 10 April 2014. Web. 19 November 2015. <http://oceanservice.noaa.gov/facts/sealevel.html>

Ki-moon, Secretary General Ban. "Unsafe water kills more people than war, Ban says on World Day." UN News Centre, United Nations, 22 March 2010. Web. 19 November 2015.
<http://www.un.org/apps/news/story.asp?NewsID=34150#.VkOzedCZ5Bo>

Kinver, Mark. "2014 warmest year on record, say US researchers." Science & Environment. *BBC News*, 16 January 2015. Web. 19 November 2015.
<http://www.bbc.com/news/science-environment-30852588>

"Livestock and Landscapes." *Food and Agriculture Organization of the United Nations*, 2012. Web. 19 November 2015. <http://www.fao.org/docrep/018/ar591e/ar591e.pdf>

"Living Planet Report 2014." World Wide Fund Global, 2014. Web. 20 November 2015.
<http://wwf.panda.org/about_our_earth/all_publications/living_planet_report/>

"Living Blue Planet Report 2015: Species, habitats and human well-being." *World Wildlife Fund*, 15 September 2015. Web. 20 November 2015.
<http://www.worldwildlife.org/publications/living-blue-planet-report-2015>

Lowenberg, Olivia. "Is your soap harming sea life? Ban on microbeads gains momentum." *The Christian Science Monitor*. 19 September 2015. Web. 24 November 2015.
<http://www.csmonitor.com/Environment/2015/0919/Is-your-soap-harming-sea-life-Ban-on-microbeads-gains-momentum>

MacDonald, Fiona. "It's official: scientists say we're entering Earth's sixth mass extinction. And Humans may struggle to survive it." *Science Alert*, June 22, 2015.. Web. 19 November 2015. <http://www.sciencealert.com/it-s-official-we-re-on-the-brink-of-earth-s-sixth-mass-extinction>

Mathiesen, Karl. "Extreme weather already on increase due to climate change, study finds." *The Guardian*, 27 April 2015. Web. 19 November 2015. <http://www.theguardian.com/environment/2015/apr/27/extreme-weather-already-on-increase-due-to-climate-change-study-finds>

Medlock, Katie. "Americans are sending two times more trash to landfills than previously thought." *Inhabitat*, 28 September 2015. Web. 19 November 2015. <http://inhabitat.com/americans-are-sending-twice-as-much-trash-to-landfills-than-previously-thought/>

Metric System. *Merriam-webster Online*. N.p., n.d. Web. 8 Dec. 2015. <http://www.merriam-webster.com/mw/table/metricsy.htm>

Mirsky, Steve. "The world is fat: Obesity now outweighs hunger worldwide." *Scientific American*, 22 August 2007. Web. 19 November 2015. <http://www.scientificamerican.com/podcast/episode/8dff8662-e7f2-99df-38e67664abff1d05/>

"More than 1 billion tons of food lost or wasted every year, UN-backed report finds." *News Centre. United Nations*, 11 May 2011. Web. 19 November 2015. <http://www.un.org/apps/news/story.asp?NewsID=38344#.VkQJgtCZ5Bo>

Newbold, Tim, Hudson, Lawrence N., Phillips, Helen R.P., Hill, Samantha L.L., Contu, Sara, Lysenko, Igor, Blandon, Abigayil, Butchart, Stuart H.M., Booth, Hollie L., Day, Julie, De Palma, Adriana, Harrison, Michelle L.K., Kirpatrick, Lucinda, Pynegar, Edwin, Robinson, Alexandra, Simpson, Jake, Mace, Georgina M., Scharlemann, Jörn P.W., Purvis, Andy. "A global model of the response of tropical and sub-tropical forest biodiveristy to anthropogenic pressures." *Pro. R. Soc. B* **281**: 20141371, August 20, 2014. Web. 19 November 2015. Web. <http://dx.doi.org/10.1098/rspb.2014.1371>

Nieuwenhuljsen, M.J., Basagaña, X., Dadvand, P. Martinez, D. Cirach, M. Beelen, R, Jacquemin, B. "Air pollution and human fertility rates." *U.S. National Library of Medicine National Institutes of Health*. Environ Int. 2014 Sep;70:9-14. Web. 19 November 2015. <http://www.ncbi.nlm.nih.gov/pubmed/24879367>

"Obesity and overweight." *World Health Organization, Media Centre*, January 2015. Web. 24 November 2015. <http://www.who.int/mediacentre/factsheets/fs311/en/>

Parigiani, Jacopo, Spooner, Samantha. "2015 is the 'Year of Soils.' Here are the 6 chilling facts every African should be aware of." *Mail & Guardian Africa*, 9 January 2015. Web. 19 November 2015. <http://mgafrica.com/article/2015-01-08-2015-is-the-year-of-soil-10-reasons-why-every-african-should-care>

"Particle Pollution." *American Lung Association, State of the Air. Health Risks*, 2013. Web. 19 November 2015. <http://www.stateoftheair.org/2013/health-risks/health-risks-particle.html>

Pedersen, M. Giorgis-Allemand, L., Bernard, C. Aguiler, I., Andersen, A.M., Ballester, F. Beelen, R.M., Chatzi, L., Cirach, M., Danileviciute, A., Dedele, A., Eijsden, Mv., Estarlich, M., Fernández-Somoano, A., Fernández, M.F., Forastiere, F., Gehring, U., Grazuleviciene, R., Gruzieva, O., Heude, B., Hoek,

G., de Hoogh, K., van den Hooven, E.H., Håberg, S,E., Jaddoe, V.W., Klümper, C., Korek. M, Krämer, U., Lerchundi, A., Lepeule, J., Nafstad, P., Nystad, W., Patelarou, E., Porta, D., Postma, D., Raaschou-Nielsen, O., Rudnai, P., Sunyer, J., Stephanou, E., Sørensen, M., Thiering, E., Tuffnell, D., Varró, M.J., Vrijkotte, T.G., Wijga, A., Wilhelm, M., Wright, J., Nieuwenhuijsen, M.J., Pershagen, G., Brunekreef, B., Kogevinas, M., Slama, R. "Ambient air pollution and low birthweight: a European cohort study (ESCAPE)." *US National Library of Medicine National Institutes of Health, Lancet Respir Med.* 2013 Nov;1(9):695-704. Web. 19 November 2015. <http://www.ncbi.nlm.nih.gov/pubmed/24429273>

Powell, Jon T., Townsend, Timothy G., Zimmerman, Julie B. "Estimates of solid waste disposal rates and reduction targets for landfill gas emissions." *Nature Climate Change*, 21 September 2015. Web. 19 November 2015. <http://www.nature.com/nclimate/journal/vaop/ncurrent/full/nclimate2804.html>

Pozzer, A., Zimmermann, P., Doering, U.M., van Aardenne, J., Tost, H., Dentener, F., Janssens-Maenhout, G., Lelieveld, J. "Effects of business-as-usual anthropogenic emissions on air quality." *Max-Planck-Gessschaft*, 1 August 2012. Atmos. Chem. Phys. Discuss., 12, 8617-8676, DOI: 10.5194/acpd-12-8617-2012, 201. Web. 19 November 2015. <https://www.mpg.de/5928050/global_air-pollution>

"Record greenhouse gas levels impact atmosphere and oceans." Press Release No. 1002. *World Meteorological Organization*, 9 September 2014. Web. 20 November 2015. <https://www.wmo.int/pages/mediacentre/press_releases/pr_1002_en.html>

Rosenberg, Matt. "Current world population." *About Education*, n.d. Web. 19 November 2015. <http://geography.about.com/od/obtainpopulationdata/a/worldpopulation.htm>

Rosenberg, Matt. "Population growth rates." *About Education*, n.d. Web. 19 November 2015. <http://geography.about.com/od/populationgeography/a/populationgrow.htm>

Schiller, Ben. "A massive global map of where all the cattle, pigs, and other livestock live." *Fast Company*, n.d. Web. 27 October 2015. <http://www.fastcoexist.com/3031945/a-massive-global-map-of-where-all-the-cattle-pigs-and-other-livestock-live>

"Statistics on literacy." *Unesco*, n.d. Web. 19 November 2015. <http://www.unesco.org/new/en/education/themes/education-building-blocks/literacy/resources/statistics>

Sullivan, Colin, ClimateWire. "Human population growth creeps back up." *Scientific American*, 14 June 2013. Web. 19 November 2015. <http://www.scientificamerican.com/article/human-population-growth-creeps-back-up/ *Reprinted from Climatewire with permission from Environment & Energy Publishing, LLC. www. eenews.net, 202-628-6500>*

Taylor, Victoria. "Microbeads causing major damage to waterways, marine life." *New York Daily News*, 24 June 2014. Web. 24 November 2015. <http://www.nydailynews.com/life-style/microbeads-causing-major-damage-waterways-marine-life-article-1.1843474>

"The garbage patch territory turns into a new state." *Unesco, office in Venice*, 4 November 2013. Web. 19 November 2015. <http://www.unesco.org/new/en/venice/about-this-office/single-view/news/the_garbage_patch_territory_turns_into_a_new_state/#.VkQCQtCZ5B>

"Threats—Deforestation." *World Wildlife Fund*, n.d. Web. 20 November 2015.
    <http://www.worldwildlife.org/threats/deforestation>

"Threats—Water scarcity." *World Wildlife Fund*, 2015. Web. 20 November 2015.
    <http://www.worldwildlife.org/threats/water-scarcity>

Vaughn, Adam. "One in six of world's species faces extinction due to climate change study." *The Guardian*,
    30 April 2015. Web. 20 November 2015.
    <http://www.theguardian.com/environment/2015/apr/30/one-in-six-of-worlds-species-faces-extinction-
    due-to-climate-change-study>

Veras, N.M., Caldini, E.G., Dolhnikoff, M., Saldiva, P. H. "Air pollution and effects on reproductive-system
    functions globally with particular emphasis on the Brazilian population." *U.S. National Library of
    Medicine, National Institutes of Health*, J Toxicol Environ Health B Crit Rev. 2010 Jan;13(1):1-15.
    Web. 20 November 2015. <http://www.ncbi.nlm.nih.gov/pubmed/20336577>

Vidal, John. "WHO: air pollution 'is single biggest environmental health risk.'" *The Guardian*, 25 March
    2014. Web. 20 November 2015.
    <http://www.theguardian.com/environment/2014/mar/25/air-pollution-single-biggest-environmental-
    health-risk-who>

Warren, R., Vanderwal, J., Price, J., Welbergen, J.A., Atkinson, I., Ramirez-Villega, J. "Quantifying the benefit
    of early climate change mitigation in avoiding biodiversity loss." *Nature Climate Change*, 12 May 2013.
    07/2013; 3-678-682. DOI: 10.1038/nclimate1887. 22 October 2015. Web. 20 November 2015.
    <http://www.researchgate.net/publication/270161032_Quantifying_the_benefit_of_early_climate_
    change_mitigation_in_avoiding_biodiversity_loss>

"Water consumed this year." *Worldometers*, 2015. Web. 20 November 2015.
    <http://www.worldometers.info/water/>

"Water news: climate change & water." *Food and Agriculture Organization of the United Nations*, n.d. Web.
    25 October 2015. http://www.fao.org/nr/water/news/clim-change.html

"Water-related diseases." *Water Sanitation Health*. World Health Organization, n.d. Web. 20 November 2015.
    <http://www.who.int/water_sanitation_health/diseases/diarrhoea/en/>

"Water Quality." International Decade for Action 'Water for Life' 2005–2015. *United Nations Department of
    Economic and Social Affairs (UNDESA)*, 23 October 2014. Web. 20 November 2015.
    <http://www.un.org/waterforlifedecade/quality.shtml>

"Water trivia facts." *United States Environmental Protection Agency*, 20 January 2015. Web. 20 November
    2015. <http://water.epa.gov/learn/kids/drinkingwater/water_trivia_facts.cfm>

Weight. *Merriam-webster Online*. N.p., n.d. Web. 8 Dec. 2015.
    <http://www.merriam-webster.com/table/dict/weight.htm>

"WEO 2014 Biomass database." World Energy Outlook. *International Energy Agency*, 2014. Web. 19
    November 2015.
    <http://www.worldenergyoutlook.org/resources/energydevelopment/energyaccessdatabase/>

"WEO 2014 Electricity database." World Energy Outlook. *International Energy Agency*, 2014. Web. 19 November 2015.
<http://www.worldenergyoutlook.org/resources/energydevelopment/energyaccessdatabase/>

"Why water? ...the numbers." Facts about Water: Statistics of the water. *The Water Project*, 12 August 2014. Web. 19 November 2015. <http://thewaterproject.org/water_stats>

"World hunger falls, but 805 million still chronically undernourished." *Food and Agriculture Organization of the United Nations*, 16 September 2014. Web. 19 November 2015.
<http://www.fao.org/news/story/en/item/243839/icode/>

Worm, B., Barbier, E.B., Beaumont, N., Duffy, J.D., Folke, C., Halpern, B.S., Jackson, J.B.C., Lotze, H.K., Micheli, F., Palumbi, S.R., Sala, E. Selkoe, K.A., Stachowicz, J.J., Watson, R. "Impacts of biodiversity loss on ocean ecoystem services." *Science*, 3 November 2006. Vol. 314 no. 5800 pp. 787-790. DOI: 10.1126/science.1132294. Web. 19 November 2015.
<https://www.sciencemag.org/content/314/5800/787>

Chapter 3

Attenborough, Sir David. "How many people can live on planet earth?" *BBC Horizon*, 2009. Web. November 20, 2015. Interview.
<http://bigthink.com/words-of-wisdom/david-attenborough-humans-arent-good-at-thinking-about-our-species-as-a-whole>

"Ban on microbeads offers best chance to protect oceans, aquatic species." Phys.org, 16 September 2015. Web. 24 November 2015.
<http://phys.org/news/2015-09-microbeads-chance-oceans-aquatic-species.html>

Bateson, Gregory. "An ecology of mind for a complex world with Nora Bateson." *The Beyond Partnership*, 2015. Web. 11 October 2015.
<http://spiraldynamics.org/wp-content/uploads/2014/12/Nora-Bateson-v6.pdf>

Boulding, Kenneth. "The economics of the coming Spaceship Earth." *Resources for the Future Forum on Environmental Quality in a Growing Economy.* Washington D.C. 8 Mar. 1966. Lecture.

"California agricultural production statistics." California Department of Food and Agriculture. Web. 24 November 2015. https://www.cdfa.ca.gov/statistics

Einstein, Albert. BrainyQuote.com. *Xplore Inc*, 2015. 11 October 2015. Web.
<http://www.brainyquote.com/quotes/quotes/a/alberteins145949.html>

"The science behind reinventing fire: transportation." Rocky Mountain Institute, n.d. Web. 24 November 2015. <http://www.rmi.org/Transportation>

"Half of global population will live in cities by end of this year, predicts UN." *United Nations News Centre*, 26 February 2008. Web. 24 November. <http://www.un.org/apps/news/story.asp?NewsID=25762>

Hall, N.M., Berry, K.L.E., Rintoul, L., Hoogenboom, M.O. Microplastic ingestion by scleractinian corals. *SpringerLink, Marine Biology*, March 2015, Volume 162, Issue 3, 725-732. First online: 04 February 2015. Web. 24 November 2015. <http://link.springer.com/article/10.1007/s00227-015-2619-7>

Hays, Jeffery. "Urban life and rural life in the developing world." *Facts and Details*, January 2012. Web. 24 November 2015. <http://factsanddetails.com/world/cat57/sub379/item2171.html>

His Royal Highness Charles, Prince of Wales. "Prince Charles shows down-to-earth side." *NBC Nightly News*, 2010. Interview. <http://www.nbcnews.com/video/nightly-news/40281801#40281801>

"Human population: population growth." Population Reference Bureau, n.d. Web. 24 November. <http://www.prb.org/Publications/Lesson-Plans/HumanPopulation/PopulationGrowth.aspx>

Jaffe, Eric. "How a quick glimpse of nature can make you more productive." *CITYLAB*, 5 May 2015. Web. 24 November 2015. <http://www.citylab.com/design/2015/05/how-a-quick-glimpse-of-nature-can-make-you-more-productive/392360>

Knapton, Sarah. "Bees contribute more to British economy than Royal Family." *The Telegraph*, 17 June 2015. Web. 24 November 2015. <http://www.telegraph.co.uk/news/earth/wildlife/11679210/Bees-contribute-more-to-British-economy-than-Royal-Family.html>

Lowenberg, Olivia. "Is your soap harming sea life? Ban on microbeads gains momentum." *The Christian Science Monitor*. 19 September 2015. Web. 24 November 2015. <http://www.csmonitor.com/Environment/2015/0919/Is-your-soap-harming-sea-life-Ban-on-microbeads-gains-momentum>

Mau, Bruce. "Massive change: The future of global design." *Bruce Mau and the Institute without Boundaries*, 2004-2005. Exhibition.

Mau, Bruce. AZ Quotes. (n.d.). Web. November 20, 2015. <http://www.azquotes.com/quote/822625>

McLuhan, Marshall. BrainyQuote.com. *Xplore Inc*, 2015. Web. 11 October 2015. <http://www.brainyquote.com/quotes/quotes/m/marshallmc130541.html>

Muir, John. My First Summer in the Sierra. *Houghtin Mifflin Company*, 1911 (110). Web. November 20, 2015. <http://vault.sierraclub.org/john_muir_exhibit/writings/my_first_summer_in_the_sierra>

Musk, Elon BrainyQuote.com. *Xplore Inc*, 2015. Web. 11 October 2015. <http://www.brainyquote.com/quotes/quotes/e/elonmusk567256.html>

Nelson, George. *How to See*. New York: Little Brown & Company, 1977. Print.

Rosenberg, Matt. "Current world population." *About Education*, n.d. Web. 20 November 2015. <http://geography.about.com/od/obtainpopulationdata/a/worldpopulation.htm>

Saintonge, Amelie. "At what speed does the earth move around the sun? (Beginner)." *Ask an Astronomer*, n.d. Web. 24 November 2015. <http://curious.astro.cornell.edu/about-us/41-our-solar-system/the-earth/orbit/91-at-what-speed-does-the-earth-move-around-the-sun-beginner>

Sinclair, Upton. BrainyQuote.com. *Xplore Inc*, 2015. Web. 11 October 2015. <http://www.brainyquote.com/quotes/quotes/u/uptonsincl138285.html>

Suzuki, David. *The Sacred Balance: Rediscovering Our Place in Nature.* Vancouver: Greystone Books, 1997. Web. 20 November 2015. <http://www.amazon.com/Sacred-BalanceRediscoveringPlaceNature/dp/1550546910/ref=sr_1_2?ie=UTF8&qid=1448298581&sr=8-2&keywords=the+sacred+balance>

Tagore, Rabindranath. BrainyQuote.com. Xplore Inc, 2015. Web. 9 October 2015. <http://www.brainyquote.com/quotes/quotes/r/rabindrana384372.html>

Taylor, Victoria. "Microbeads causing major damage to waterways, marine life." *New York Daily News*, 24 June 2014. Web. 24 November 2015. <http://www.nydailynews.com/life-style/microbeads-causing-major-damage-waterways-marine-life-article-1.1843474>

"The economics of biophilia." *Terrapin Bright Green*, 2014. Web. 34 November 2015. <http://www.terrapinbrightgreen.com/reports/the-economics-of-biophilia>

"The Importance of olive-oil production in Italy." *Food and Agriculture Organization of the United Nations*, n.d. Web. 24 November. <ftp://ftp.fao.org/docrep/fao/009/a0007e/a0007e01.pdf>

Thompson, Andrea. "Drought takes $2.7 billion toll on California agriculture." *Climate Central*, 2 June 2015. Web. 24 November 2015. <http://www.climatecentral.org/news/drought-cost-california-agriculture-19061>

Voelcker, John. "1.2 billion vehicles on world's roads now, 2 billion by 2035: report." *Green Car Reports*, 29 July 2014. Web. November 20, 2015. <http://www.greencarreports.com/news/1093560_1-2-billion-vehicles-on-worlds-roads-now-2-billion-by-2035-report>

White, Mathew P., Alcock, Ian, Wheeler, Benedict W., Depledge, Michael H. "Would You Be Happier Living in a Greener Urban Area? A Fixed-Effects Analysis of Panel Data." *Psychological Science*, published online 23 April 2013, DOI: 10.1177/0956797612464659. <http://www.ecehh.org/research-projects/urban-green-space>

Wilson, E.O.. *Biophilia*, (1st ed.). Cambridge: Harvard University Press, 1984. Print.

"World footprint, do we fit on the planet?" Global Footprint Network. World Footprint, 20 November 2015. Web. 23 November 2015. <http://www.footprintnetwork.org/en/index.php/GFN/page/world_footprint>

Chapter 4

Baraniuk, Chris. "The Devonian extinction saw the oceans choke to death." *BBC Earth*. 23 June 2015. Web. 23 November 2015. <http://www.bbc.com/earth/story/20150624-the-day-the-oceans-died>

Choi, Charles Q. "Extreme global warming may have caused largest extinction ever." *Live science*, 18 October 2012. Web. 23 November 2015. <http://www.livescience.com/24091-extreme-global-warming-mass-extinction.html>

"Clothes for a change: background info." Organic Consumers Organization. Web. 23 November 2015. <https://www.organicconsumers.org/old_articles/clothes/background.php>

"Cold War: A Brief History—Nuclear Deterrence." *Atomic archive.com*, n.d. Web. 24 November 2015.
   <http://www.atomicarchive.com/History/coldwar/page15.shtml>

Diaz, B., Rosenberg, R. "Dead Zones." *VIMS. Virgina Institute of Marine Science*, n.d. Web. 22 October
   2015. <http://www.vims.edu/research/topics/dead_zones/index.php>

"Earth expected to be habitable for another 1.75 billion years." *Science News*, 18 September 2013. Web.
   November 2015. <http://www.sciencedaily.com/releases/2013/09/130918211434.htm>

"Earth's mass extinctions." Timeline, 23 September 2015. Web. 23 November 2015.
   <https://www.timeline.com/stories/mass-extinctions>

"End Triassic extinction." Encyclopaedia Britannica, 4 March 2014. Web. 23 November 2015.
   <http://www.britannica.com/science/end-Triassic-extinction>

Gerken, James. "2014 Was The Hottest Year Since At Least 1880, Government Finds." *Huffington Post*. 16
   January 2015. Web. 24 November 2015.
   <http://www.huffingtonpost.com/2015/01/16/2014-hottest-year-on-record_n_6479896.html>

"Global Carbon Budget." *Carbon Project*, n.d. Web. 23 November 2015.
   <http://www.globalcarbonproject.org/carbonbudget/14/hl-full.htm>

Jefferson, Thomas" *Regulations.gov*, n.d. Web. 15 October 2015
   <http://www.regulations.gov/#!documentDetail;D=FHWA-2013-0002-0175>

Lincoln, Abraham. *Goodreads*, n.d. Web. 23 November 2015.
   <http://www.goodreads.com/quotes/31631-we-are-not-enemies-but-friends-we-must-not-be>

Newton, Steven. "How old is the Earth." *National Center for Science Education*, 17 October 2008.
   <http://ncse.com/evolution/science/how-old-is-earth>

Paine, Thomas. BrainyQuote.com. *Xplore Inc,*, 2015. Web. 24 November 2015.
   <http://www.brainyquote.com/quotes/quotes/t/thomaspain159470.html>

"Permian mass extinction." Prehistoric Life. *BBC Nature*, October 2014.
   <http://www.bbc.co.uk/nature/extinction_events/Permian–Triassic_extinction_event>

President Theodore Roosevelt. The Foundations. The National Museum of American History, Smithsonian.
   Web 23 November 2015. <http://americanhistory.si.edu/presidency/2b7c.html>

"Product gallery; cotton" Water Footprint Network, n.d. Web. November 23 2015.
   <http://waterfootprint.org/en/resources/interactive-tools/product-gallery>

Rummage, Timothy. Personal comment.

Salk, Jonas. Big Think, n.d. Web. 23 November 2015.
   <http://bigthink.com/words-of-wisdom/jonas-salk-on-humanitys-greatest-responsibility>

"The Archean: The first life on earth." *Smithsonian Museum of Natural History*, n.d. Web. 23 November 2015.
   <http://paleobiology.si.edu/geotime/main/htmlversion/archean3.html>

Thoreau, H.D. Goodreads, n.d. Web. 23 November 2015.
<http://www.goodreads.com/quotes/217353-what-s-the-use-of-a-fine-house-if-you-haven-t>

Twain, Mark. BrainyQuote.com. *Xplore Inc*, 2015. 24 November 2015.
<http://www.brainyquote.com/quotes/quotes/m/marktwain109624.html>

"Using, sharing, new technologies is key for conservation." *ScienceDaily*, 5 October 2015. Web. 23 November 2015. <www.sciencedaily.com/releases/2015/10/151005184528.htm>

"What is ocean acidification: the chemistry." *NOAA PMEL Carbon Program*, n.d. Web. 23 November 2015.
<http://www.pmel.noaa.gov/co2/story/What+is+Ocean+Acidification%3F>

Wilson, Edward O. The social conquest of earth. Quote of Stephen Greenblatt. New York: Liveright Pbulishing Corporation, 2012. Web. 25 November 2015.
<http://books.wwnorton.com/books/detail.aspx?ID=4294972295>

Chapter 5

Bard, Carl. Keepinspiring.me, n.d. Web. 23 November 2015.
<http://www.keepinspiring.me/famous-quotes-about-success>

Cox, Wendell. Largest 1,000 cities on earth: world urban areas: 2015 edition. *New Geography*, 2 February 2015. Web. 23 November 2015.
<http://www.newgeography.com/content/004841-largest-1000-cities-earth-world-urban-areas-2015-edition>

"Current world population." *Worldometers*, 2015. Web. 20 November 2015.
<http://www.worldometers.info/world-population/>

Drucker, Peter F. Goodreads, n.d. Web. 23 November 2015.
<http://www.goodreads.com/quotes/420819-if-you-want-something-new-you-have-to-stop-doing>

"In 2015, Earth Overshoot Day lands on August 13." Earth Overshoot Day 2015, 2015. Web. 20 November 2015. Web. <http://www.overshootday.org>

Geiling, Esri, Geiling, Natasha. "Make cities explode in size with these interactive maps." *Smithsonian*, 30 September 30, 2014. Web. 23 November 2015.
<http://www.smithsonianmag.com/science-nature/make-cities-explode-size-these-interactive-maps-180952832/?no-ist>

Rosenberg, Matt. "Current world population." *About education*, n.d. Web. 20 November 2015.
<http://geography.about.com/od/obtainpopulationdata/a/worldpopulation.htm>

Stamp, Josiah Charles. Goodreads, n.d. Web. 23 November 2015.
<http://www.goodreads.com/quotes/384775-it-is-easy-to-dodge-our-responsibilities-but-we-cannot>

"The growth of the automobile." Scientific American,Vol. 122. Scientific American, 1920. Web. 23 November 2015.
<https://books.google.com/books?id=w8QxAQAAMAAJ&pg=PA3&lpg=PA3&dq=3+million+cars+in+1915&source=bl&ots=YANfRFXXAc&sig=-EAwgQMYJ5zAyxkz1tFcX0cmhxA&hl=en&sa=X&ved=0CCMQ6AEwATgKahUKEwjv_ZTY6o3JAhWM5SYKHaAiD14#v=onepage&q=3%20million%20cars%20in%201915&f=false>

"transformation." Def. 3. *Dictionary.com Unabridged*. Random House, Inc. Web. 15 Oct. 2015.
Dictionary.com <http://dictionary.reference.com/browse/transformation.>

Voelcker, John. "1.2 Billion Vehicles On World's Roads Now, 2 Billion By 2035: Report." *Green Car Reports*, 29 July 2014. Web. November 20, 2015.
<http://www.greencarreports.com/news/1093560_1-2-billion-vehicles-on-worlds-roads-now-2-billion-by-2035-report>

"World footprint, do we fit on the planet?" Global Footprint Network. World Footprint, 20 November 2015.
Web. 23 November 2015. <http://www.footprintnetwork.org/en/index.php/GFN/page/world_footprint>

Chapter 6

"Climate Change and National security in 2014 Quadrennial Defense Review." The Center for Climate and Security, n.d. Web. 24 November 2015.
<http://climateandsecurity.org/2014/03/04/climate-change-and-national-security-in-the-2014-quadrennial-defense-review>

Houle, David. Entering the Shift Age: *The End of the Information Age and the New Era of Transformation*. Naperville: Sourcebooks, 2012. Print.

Inman, Mason. "Carbon is forever." *Nature Reports, Climate Change*. 20 November 2008. doi:10.1038/climate.2008.122. Web. 24 November 2015.
<http://www.nature.com/climate/2008/0812/full/climate.2008.122.html>

McKibben, Bill. "Remember This: 350 Parts Per Million." *The Washington Post*, 28 December 2007. Web. 24 November. 2015.
<http://www.washingtonpost.com/wp-dyn/content/article/2007/12/27/AR2007122701942.html>

SmarterSafter. "Bracing for the Storm." Smartersafer.org, 2015. Web. 24 November 2015.
<http://www.smartersafer.org/wp-content/uploads/Bracing-for-the-Storm.pdf>

"Sustainable Innovation Forum 2015." *UNEP, Climate Action*, 2015. Web. 24 November 2015.
<http://www.cop21paris.org>

"Trends in Global CO2 Emissions, 2013 Report." PBL Netherlands Environmental Assessment Agency, 2013. Web. 24 November 2015.
<http://edgar.jrc.ec.europa.eu/news_docs/pbl-2013-trends-in-global-co2-emissions-2013-report-1148.pdf>

Tverberg, Gail. "World Energy Consumption Since 1820 in Charts." Our Finite World, 12 March 2012. Web. 24 November 2015.
<http://ourfiniteworld.com/2012/03/12/world-energy-consumption-since-1820-in-charts>

"What the world needs to watch." Annual Data/Atmospheric CO_2. CO_2 *Now.org*, n.d. Web 24 November 2015.
<http://co2now.org/current-co2/co2-now/annual-co2.html>

"World Climate Conference." World Meteorological Organization, n.d. Web. 24 November 2015.
<https://www.wmo.int/pages/themes/climate/international_wcc.php>

Chapter 7

"Carbon Cycle Science." NOAA Earth Systems Research Laboratory, n.d. Web. 24 November 2015.
    <http://www.esrl.noaa.gov/research/themes/carbon>

"Effects of Changing the Carbon Cycle." NASA Earth Observatory, n.d. Web. 24 November 2015.
    <http://earthobservatory.nasa.gov/Features/CarbonCycle/page5.php>

Einstein, Albert. BrainyQuote.com. *Xplore Inc*, 2015. Web. 24 November 2015.
    <http://www.brainyquote.com/quotes/quotes/a/alberteins385842.html>

Kennedy, John Fitzgerald. "Nasa Moon Landing." John F. Kennedy Presidential Library and Museum, n.d.
    Web. 24 November 2015.
    <http://www.jfklibrary.org/JFK/JFK-Legacy/NASA-Moon-Landing.aspx>

King, Jr., Martin Luther. "MLK Quote of the week: times of challenge and controversy." The King Center, 19
    September 2015. Web. 24 November 2015.
    <http://www.thekingcenter.org/blog/mlk-quote-week-times-challenge-and-controversy>

Maathai, Wangari. BrainyQuote.com. *Xplore Inc*, 2015. Web. 24 November 2015.
    <http://www.brainyquote.com/quotes/quotes/w/wangarimaa416623.html>

Mellgard, Peter. "The Marshall Islands 'Will Go Under' if the Paris climate talks fail, foreign minister [Tony
    de Brum] says." *The World Post*, 30 September 2015. Web. 24 November.
    <http://www.huffingtonpost.com/entry/marshall-islands-paris-climate_560a9784e4b0dd8503091e6c>

Olmstead, Frederick Law (maxbobinski). "The rights of prosperity are more important than the desires of the
    present." *Tweet*, n.d. Web. 24 November 2015.
    <https://twitter.com/maxbobinski/status/447925621511819265>

Professor Dumbledore. "The 5 wisest Dumbledore quotes in a Harry Potter film." Reel Life Wisdom, n.d.
    Web. 24 November 2015.
    <http://www.reellifewisdom.com/top_five_wisest_dumbledore_quotes_in_a_harry_potter_film>

Salatin, Joel. Food, Inc. *IMBD*, 2008. Web. 24 November 2015. http://www.imdb.com/title/tt1286537/quotes

"Two degrees: The history of climate changes speed limit." *Carbon Brief*, 8 December 2014. Web. 24
    November 2015.
    <http://www.carbonbrief.org/two-degrees-the-history-of-climate-changes-speed-limit>

van Gogh, Vincent. *Goodreads*, n.d. Web. 24 November 2015.
    <http://www.goodreads.com/quotes/66097-what-would-life-be-if-we-had-no-courage-to>

Zen Buddhists. *Motivational Quotes About*, n.d. Web. 24 November 2015.
    <http://www.motivationalquotesabout.com/future?page=4>

Chapter 8

Attenborough, Sir David. "How many people can live on planet earth?" *BBC Horizon*, 2009. Web. November
    20, 2015. Interview.
    <http://bigthink.com/words-of-wisdom/david-attenborough-humans-arent-good-at-thinking-about-our-
    species-as-a-whole>

Brown, Lester. "Lester Brown&#29;s Plan B: Mobilizing to save civilization." Nature and Environment. *Mother Earth News*, 29 October 2010. Web. 20 November 2015. <http://www.motherearthnews.com/nature-and-environment/lester-brown-zboz10zkon.aspx>

"Car emissions and global warming." *Union of Concerned Scientists*, n.d. Web. November 20, 2015. <http://www.ucsusa.org/clean-vehicles/car-emissions-and-global-warming#.VkWWNNCZ5Bo>

Carson, Rachel. Silent Spring. Goodreads, 1962. Web. 20 November 2015. <http://www.goodreads.com/quotes/836395-we-stand-now-where-two-roads-diverge-but-unlike-the>

"Estimating U.S. Government Subsidies to Energy Sources: 2002-2008." *Environmental Law Institute*, 2009. Web. 20 November 2015. <https://www.eli.org/sites/default/files/eli-pubs/d19_07.pdf>

"Global Emissions by Gas." Global Greenhouse Gas Emissions Data. *United States Environmental Protection Agency*. Overview of Greenhouse Gases, n.d. Web. 20 November 2015. <http://www3.epa.gov/climatechange/ghgemissions/global.html.>

"Global strategic trends—out to 2045." Strategic Trends Programme (5th ed.). *Ministry of Defence*, 2014. Web. 20 November 2015. <https://www.gov.uk/government/uploads/system/uploads/attachment_data/file/348164/20140821_DCDC_GST_5_Web_Secured.pdf>

Houle, David. *Entering the Shift Age: The End of the Information Age and the New Era of Transformation.* Sourcebooks, 2012. Print.

"In 2015, Earth Overshoot Day lands on August 13." *Earth Overshoot Day 2015*, 2015. Web. 20 November 2015. <http://www.overshootday.org>

Kennedy, John Fitzgerald. *John F. Kennedy Moon Speech—Rice University Stadium*, 12 September 1962. Web. 20 November 2015. <http://er.jsc.nasa.gov/seh/ricetalk.htm>

Johnson, Terrell. "Climate change warning: 20 cities with the most to lose from rising seas." *The Weather Channel*, 28 August 2013. Web. 20 November 2015. <http://www.weather.com/science/environment/news/20-cities-most-lose-rising-sea-levels-20130822?pageno=2#/5>

Living Blue Planet Report 2015: Species, habitats and human well-being. *World Wildlife Fund*, 15 September 2015. Web. 20 November 2015. <http://www.worldwildlife.org/publications/living-blue-planet-report-2015>

Matthews, Christopher. "Livestock a major threat to environment." *FAOnewsroom*, 29 November 2006.Web. 20 November 2015. <http://www.fao.org/newsroom/en/News/2006/1000448/index.html>

McMahon, Jeff. "Elon Musk: Tesla powerpack doesn't need renewables, Battery Market 'Staggeringly Gigantic.'" *Forbes/Tech*, 5 August 2015. Web. 20 November 2015. <http://www.forbes.com/sites/jeffmcmahon/2015/08/05/elon-musk-tesla-powerpack-doesnt-need-renewables-battery-market-staggeringly-gigantic/>

"National Security implications of climate-related risks and a changing climate." *Department of Defense*, 23 July 2015. Web. 20 November 2015. <http://archive.defense.gov/pubs/150724-congressional-report-on-national-implications-of-climate-change.pdf?source=govdelivery>

"Overview of greenhouse gasses." Carbon Dioxide Emissions." *United States Environmental Protection Agency*, n.d. Web. 20 November 2015. <http://www3.epa.gov/climatechange/ghgemissions/gases/co2.html.>

Reagan, Ronald. BrainyQuote.com. *Xplore Inc*, 2015. Web. 23 November 2015 <http://www.brainyquote.com/quotes/quotes/r/ronaldreag147717.html>

"Sylvia Earle." BrainyQuote.com. *Xplore Inc*, 2015. 23 November 2015. Web. <http://www.brainyquote.com/quotes/quotes/s/sylviaearl412315.html>

Toffler, Alvin. *Goodreads*, n.d. Web. 20 November 2015. <https://www.goodreads.com/author/quotes/3030.Alvin_Toffler>

Voelcker, John. "1.2 billion vehicles on world's roads now, 2 billion by 2035: Report." *Green Car Reports*, 29 July 2014. Web. November 20, 2015. <http://www.greencarreports.com/news/1093560_1-2-billion-vehicles-on-worlds-roads-now-2-billion-by-2035-report>

"Why the building sector." Architecture 2030. *2013 2030 Inc.*, 2012. Web. 20 November 2015. <http://architecture2030.org/buildings_problem_why>

"Winston Churchill." Philosiblog, 28 May 2012. 20 November 2015. Web. <http://philosiblog.com/2012/05/28/sometimes-it-is-not-enough-to-do-our-best-we-must-do-what-is-required>

Chapter 9

Aubrey, Allison. "It's time to get serious about reducing food waste, Fed say." The Salt. *NPR. Morning Edition*,16 September 2015. Web. 20 November 2015. <http://www.npr.org/sections/thesalt/2015/09/16/440825159/its-time-to-get-serious-about-reducing-food-waste-feds-say>

"Ban on microbeads offers best chance to protect oceans, aquatic species." Phys.org, 16 September 2015. Web. 24 November 2015. <http://phys.org/news/2015-09-microbeads-chance-oceans-aquatic-species.html>

Berry, Thomas. The Great Work: our way into the future. *Bell Tower*, 1999. Web. 23 November 2015. <http://www.earthlaws.org.au/events/wild-law-judgment-project>

Brown, Lester. Lester Brown&#29;s Plan B: Mobilizing to Save Civilization. Nature and Environment. Mother Earth News, 29 October 2010. Web. 20 November 2015. <http://www.motherearthnews.com/nature-and-environment/lester-brown-zboz10zkon.aspx>

Bryant, William Jennings. *Goodreads*, n.d. Web. 20 November 2015. <http://www.goodreads.com/quotes/41911-destiny-is-not-a-matter-of-chance-it-is-a>

Dumas, Andre. Geist, Dr. Philip R. The Three Musketeers. *OcalaStarBanner.*, 20 December 2009. Web. 20 November 2015. <http://pgeist.blogs.ocala.com/10023/unus-pro-omnibus-omnes-pro-uno>

"EWG lauds proposed curbs on chemical industry secrecy." Environmental Working Group, 12 October 2010. Web. 20 November 2015. <http://www.ewg.org/Comments-on-TSCA-Inventory-Update-Reporting>

Hoffman, Beth. The shocking cost of food waste. Forbes, 11 April 2014. Web. 20 November 2015. <http://www.forbes.com/sites/bethhoffman/2014/04/11/the-shocking-cost-of-food-waste>

King, Jr., Martin Luther. Letter from a Birmingham Jail [King, Jr.]. African Studies Center, University of Pennyslvania, 1963. Web. 20 November 2015. <https://www.africa.upenn.edu/Articles_Gen/Letter_Birmingham.html>

King, Jr., Martin Luther. Strength to Love, 1963. Web. 20 November 2015. <http://pixeljoint.com/pixels/quotes.asp?pid=1004>

Larkin, Amy. Environmental debt: the hidden costs of changing global economy. New York: St Martin's Press, 2013. Web. 20 November 2015. <http://www.amazon.com/Environmental-Debt-Hidden-Changing-Economy/dp/1137279206>

Lipinski, Brian, et al. "Reducing food loss and food waste: Creating a sustainable food future, installment II." World Resources Institute, 2013. Web. 20 November 2015. <http://www.wri.org/publication/reducing-food-loss-and-waste>

Lowenberg, Olivia. "Is your soap harming sea life? Ban on microbeads gains momentum." *The Christian Science Monitor.* 19 September 2015. Web. 24 November 2015. <http://www.csmonitor.com/Environment/2015/0919/Is-your-soap-harming-sea-life-Ban-on-microbeads-gains-momentum>

McDonough, William. Address to the Woods Hole Symposium. McDonough Innovation, 2003. Web. 20 November 2015. <http://www.mcdonough.com/speaking-writing/address-to-the-woods-hole-symposium/#.Vk942tCZ5Bo>

"Noblesse Oblige." Cambridge Advanced Learners Dictionary & Thesaurus. Cambridge: Cambridge University Press, n.d. Web. 13 October 2015. <http://dictionary.cambridge.org/us/dictionary/english/noblesse-oblige>

"Plastic Grocery Bags: How long until they decompose?" *Business Ethics, The Magazine of Corporate Responsibility*, 2010. Web. 20 November 2015. <http://business-ethics.com/2010/09/17/4918-plastic-grocery-bags-how-long-until-they-decompose/.>

Plumer, Brad. "How the US manages to waster $165 billion in food each year." *The Washington Post*, August 22, 2012. Web. 20 November 2015. <https://www.washingtonpost.com/news/wonk/wp/2012/08/22/how-food-actually-gets-wasted-in-the-united-states>

"Recycling Basics." *United States Environmental Protection Agency*, n.d. Web. 20 November 20 2015. <http://www.mrra.net/wp-content/uploads/Why-Recycle.pdf>

Roosevelt, Theodore. BrainyQuote.com. *Xplore Inc*, 2015. Web. 23 November 2015.
<http://www.brainyquote.com/quotes/quotes/t/theodorero100965.html>

Roosevelt, Theodore. *The American History Museum, Smithsonian*, 1907. Web. 20 November 2015.
<http://americanhistory.si.edu/presidency/2b7c.html>

Shiva, Vandana. *Goodreads*, n.d. Web. 20 November 2015.
<http://www.goodreads.com/quotes/98780-in-nature-s-economy-the-currency-is-not-money-it-is>

Sydenham, Thomas. "Primum non nocere." *US National Library of Medicine, National Institute of Health*.
Web. 13 October 2015. <http://www.ncbi.nlm.nih.gov/pubmed/15778417>

Taylor, Victoria. "Microbeads causing major damage to waterways, marine life." *New York Daily News*, 24
June 2014. Web. 24 November 2015.
<http://www.nydailynews.com/life-style/microbeads-causing-major-damage-waterways-marine-life-article-1.1843474>

The Dalai Lama. *Goodreads*, n.d. Web. 20 November 2015.
<http://www.goodreads.com/quotes/7777-if-you-think-you-are-too-small-to-make-a>

Thoreau, Henry David. Walden, 1966 (1)67. Original publishing 1854. Respectfully Quoted: A Dictionary
of Quotations Requested from the Congressional Research Service. *Washington D.C.: Library of
Congress*, 1989; *Bartleby.com*, 2003. Web. 20 November 2015. <www.bartleby.com/73>

"Toxic chemicals found in minority cord blood." *Environmental Working Group*, 2 December 2009. Web. 23
November 2015.
<http://www.ewg.org/news/news-releases/2009/12/02/toxic-chemicals-found-minority-cord-blood>

Turkish proverb. *Thinkexist.com*, n.d. Web. 20 November 2015.
<http://thinkexist.com/quotation/no_matter_how_far_you_have_gone_on_the_wrong_road/188749.html>

Turner, Dale.BrainyQuote.com. *Xplore Inc*, 2015. Web. 23 November 2015.
<http://www.brainyquote.com/quotes/quotes/d/daleturner121840.html>

Tzu, Lao. Catalyzing Chance. *Tao Te Ching*, n.d. Web. 20 November 2015.
<http://www.catalyzingchange.org/10-lao-tzu-quotes-for-healthy-living>

Zeitler, Ron. Personal communication to authors, n.d. Oral.

Chapter 10

Dylan, Bob. LyricsFreak.com, n.d. Web. 24 November 2015.
<http://www.lyricsfreak.com/b/bob+dylan/the+times+they+are+a+changin_20021240.html>

Jobs, Steve. "Apple Confidential—Steve Jobs on 'Think Different'—Internal Meeting Sept. 23, 1997."
Online video clip. YouTube, 23 September 1997. Web. 24 November 1997.
<https://www.youtube.com/watch?v=9GMQhOm-Dqo>

DAVID HOULE

David Houle is a futurist, strategist and speaker. Houle spent more than 20 years in media and entertainment. He worked at NBC, CBS, and was part of the senior executive team that created and launched MTV, Nickelodeon, VH1 and CNN Headline News.

Houle has won a number of awards. He won two Emmys, the prestigious George Foster Peabody award, and the Heartland award for "Hank Aaron: Chasing the Dream." He was also nominated for an Academy Award. He is the Futurist in Residence at the Ringling College of Art + Design.

He has delivered some 700 speeches on six continents and thirteen countries. He is often called "the CEOs' Futurist" having spoken to or advised 3,500+ CEOs and business owners in the past eight years.

Houle coined the phrase the Shift Age and has written extensively about the future and the future of energy. This is his seventh book.

His primary web site is www.davidhoule.com

TIM RUMAGE

Tim Rumage is a planetary ethicist and naturalist. Taking an interdisciplinary and systems thinking approach to education, he has been teaching at the intersection of Science, Ecology, Art, Design and Architecture for more than 30 years.

Tim is the Coordinator/Developer of Environmental Studies at Ringling College of Art and Design where he teaches courses on environmental science, sustainability, creating ecological cities, applied environmental design, food, water, biodiversity and environmental ethics. He is also a Coordinator for Sustainability in Design Education for CUMULUS and a frequent lecturer at other colleges and for community organizations.

As a trained field biologist, Tim has done research on Marine Mammals, Pelagic Birds, Bats, Habitat Restoration and Land Planning. He has been involved in a variety of interdisciplinary projects in the US and Africa involving habitat restoration and protection, green infrastructure, local food production and sustainability. Tim's current work focuses on the economic value of nature and nature's services.

tim@planetaryethicist.com